The

ALIEN A

A critical appraisal of th
human beings have been abducted and examined by alien
entities.

Also in this series:

The Evidence for BIGFOOT AND OTHER MAN-BEASTS
Janet and Colin Bord
The Evidence for UFOs
Hilary Evans
The Evidence for VISIONS OF THE VIRGIN MARY
Kevin McClure

In preparation:

The Evidence for GHOSTS
Andrew Green
The Evidence for PHANTOM HITCH-HIKERS
Michael Goss

The Evidence for ALIEN ABDUCTIONS

JOHN RIMMER

Series Editor: Hilary Evans

THE AQUARIAN PRESS
Wellingborough, Northamptonshire

First published 1984

British Library Cataloguing in Publication Data

Rimmer, John
The evidence for alien abductions
1. Abduction 2. Life on other planets
I. Title
362.8'8 HV6571

ISBN 0-85030-362-1

The Aquarian Press is part of the Thorsons Publishing Group

Printed and bound in Great Britain by
Whitstable Litho Ltd., Whitstable, Kent

CONTENTS

'THE EVIDENCE' Series is prepared by The Aquarian Press in collaboration with ASSAP (Association for the Scientific Study of Anomalous Phenomena) under the editorship of Hilary Evans. Each book in the series will give a comprehensive, impartial and up-to-date assessment of the evidence currently available for a particular phenomenon.

Each book is written by a recognized authority on the subject who is in a position both to give a comprehensive presentation of the facts and to analyze them in the light of his own experience and first-hand research.

ASSAP (Association for the Scientific Study of Anomalous Phenomena) was founded in 1981 to bring together people working in different fields of anomaly research. It does not compete with other societies or organizations, but serves as a link organization enabling members of existing groups to share views and information and benefit from pooled resources. ASSAP issues its own publications, has its own research archives, library and other facilities, and holds periodic public conferences and training events in various parts of the country: ASSAP co-operates with local groups or, where none exists, may form one of its own.

ASSAP members include people from all walks of life who share a belief that it is the scientific approach which is most likely to solve these enigmas: they are neither uncritical 'believers' on the one hand, nor blinkered sceptics on the other, but are ready to go where the evidence leads them. If you sympathise with this attitude and would like to participate actively in our exciting pursuit of truth, you may consider joining us. Write for fuller details to the Editor, Evidence Series, Aquarian Press, Denington Estate, Wellingborough NN8 2RQ.

ILLUSTRATIONS

*Note: Illustrations marked * have been supplied by the Mary Evans Picture Library.*

NOTE

Every specialist field tends to generate its own jargon, which can be confusing to outsiders or those new to the subject. Ufology has its own vernacular, and 'ufology' is part of it, a hybrid word to provide a convenient way of saying 'the systematic study of reports of unidentified flying objects and of the people making those reports', and that is how I shall use the word in this book.

As so little is known with absolute certainty about the UFO and abduction phenomena, much of the jargon that is used is designed to prevent too definite an attitude being inadvertently created. 'Percipient' is used instead of 'witness' – we are not sure that there was something definitely there to be witnessed; but something was 'perceived', whether it was a sighting of a physical object, or an hallucination.

Most readers will be familiar with the terminology of 'close encounters' of various kinds, if only from the well-known film. A close encounter of the third kind, in general ufological usage, is one where 'creatures', 'beings', 'entities', or whatever, are seen in conjunction with a UFO. There does not necessarily have to be any contact with the 'percipient'.

Any serious scientific report of a UFO investigation is riddled with a great number of absolutely necessary words like 'alleged', 'supposed', 'apparent' and 'reportedly'. Ufology deals with the testimony of individuals, and such caution is vital; we can assume nothing. However, they do tend to get in the way of a smooth flowing narrative, and by and large I have omitted them when summarizing cases. They should, however, be assumed in all descriptions of 'alleged' sightings.

Superior figures in the text refer to the Bibliography on page 155.

ONE: THE REPORTS

'A tired driver on a lonely road . . .' That is how a popular television programme of the 1960s began. *The Invaders* was a tautly plotted tale of one man's desperate fight to prove to a disbelieving world the reality of the threat from 'the invaders' – sinister alien forces who were plotting to take over this planet. All through his search, which lasted for quite a few highly successful series, the final piece of evidence was just ready to fall into his hands – the one definite alien specimen or artefact that no one could ignore. And always, at the last moment, that evidence would fade away, and once again Roy Thinnes would be off down that lonely road . . .

Another image from the world of entertainment: a poster for the film *Close Encounters of the Third Kind*. A deserted road stretches away, straight across a desert or empty plain. Beyond the horizon a glow begins to lighten the night sky. Is this the light of a town over the crest of a hill, or . . . ?

What is interesting about these images of popular fiction is just how close they are to the realities of the situations that UFO investigators come up against when they start looking at the experiences that have come to be known as 'UFO Abductions'.

Most UFO abductions do indeed begin on a lonely road at night, for it is a remarkable fact that the great majority of all reports of people allegedly being taken on board an alien spacecraft have started with the 'abductee' driving a car at night. Usually, before the strange events begin, there is an initial sighting of a UFO, or a glowing light on the road ahead – just like the film poster. Or a strange light, seen in the driving mirror, follows the car. By combining features that recur time and time again, we can build up a picture of a 'typical' abduction, if such a thing is conceivable. We can begin to experience, through this scenario, what it might be like if we, too, were abducted by some strange visitor from the skies.

* * * *

It is late at night. We are driving home from a visit to friends, or perhaps from a late night at work. The road is familiar – we know it well by daylight – and is just outside the suburbs of a large city. We are alone in the car. Suddenly a flashing light across a field catches our attention. It is perhaps two or three hundred yards away from us, and at first we do not pay too much attention to it; but now it seems to be getting nearer. It becomes so bright that we have difficulty concentrating on the road ahead; but then that does not seem to matter as the control of the car is removed from us. Without our help it glides to a smooth stop at the side of the road. All the lights go out and we are in total darkness. Suddenly, the blinding light appears again; strange figures, shadows, move towards us through the glare; a feeling of terror fills our mind, and we lose all consciousness.

Slowly a bright light fills our eyes once more, but this time it is above us. It is the light of a strange room, in which we are lying flat on a bed. Gradually, our eyes become adjusted to the light and we become aware of figures around us. We begin to make out their features. If we are lucky, they will look quite normal. Others have not been so lucky, and they have awoken to find themselves surrounded by shining-eyed, grotesque dwarfs, or hideous ape-like creatures, made only more terrifying by the incongruous white lab-coats they are wearing.

But our abductors are human – mostly. Their eyes are rather large, they do not seem to have much of a nose, and their mouths are lipless slits. Now we realize that they are conducting some sort of an examination of us; they are pressing an instrument against us, all over our body. It touches the back of our neck and there is a searing moment of pain. We notice, perhaps with a little embarrassment, that they seem rather interested in our genitals.

The examination is over, and we are taken from the table down a series of corridors. Strange images confront us – pictures of the Earth from space, or of our own environment. We see our car abandoned at the side of the road. Perhaps we even see our own lifeless figure slumped inside at the wheel. The images are stranger now; alien landscapes burning under some weirdly coloured sun, fantastic cityscapes of crystal towers. And suddenly that terrible image that our kind now recognizes with an almost atavistic fear – a mushroom cloud.

Suddenly, it is all over. We are back in our car, rubbing our eyes and trying to make some sense of what has happened, wondering what we should do now. Tell the police, the government . . .? We realize that they will never believe us. Or we may find ourselves wandering aimlessly down a road miles from the last place we remember; or struggling, cut and bruised, through dense undergrowth in a wood miles from the main road.

Perhaps we are sitting in our car and wondering if we shall ever be able to forget the ordeal we have been through. Or perhaps, even more frighteningly, we may be sitting there totally unable to remember a single thing that has happened to us in the last twenty-four hours.

The size of the problem

All the incidents in the foregoing scenario have been taken from accounts given by ordinary honest people who have been caught up in an alien abduction. This frightening science fiction episode is a nightmare reality for hundreds of people. Over the ten-year period 1970 to 1980 there have been about five hundred such episodes reported to UFO investigators and writers. It is probable that the number of people who have undergone this trauma and elected to keep it a close secret may be the same again. Some estimates put the total number of 'abductees', counting some multiple cases, as upwards of two thousand, world wide.

Reports coming into the specialist UFO magazines and organizations have shown a remarkable increase in the number of cases in the past four or five years. Whereas in the early 1970s the abduction scenario was confined to perhaps a dozen or so well-publicized cases, now new cases arrive in investigators' in-trays almost weekly. This fact in itself raises some very important questions. It can be argued that there has not in fact been a numerical increase in the number of people experiencing abductions, but that increased publicity has led to a 'snowball effect', whereby people are encouraged to come forward with their stories because they can now see that there are people and organizations who are willing to give them a fair hearing; as more people come forward, others are encouraged to make their experiences known. Similarly, now that investigators know of other such cases, they will begin deliberately to seek out the abduction cases amongst the reports that come their way.

Another important factor in the massive increase in the number of these cases is the growing use of 'hypnotic regression' to try and fill in the missing hours that many UFO witnesses seem to experience in their memories of their UFO adventures. Most of the more recent abduction accounts have been uncovered in this way, and we can only speculate how many other 'close encounter' stories of the 1950s and 1960s would have yielded abduction stories if this hypnotic technique had been in widespread use amongst UFO investigators of the period. But the use of hypnosis itself opens up significant questions, and it is now a major source of controversy in the UFO field, as we shall see in a later chapter.

In the typical 'hypnotic regression' case, the subject will be largely unaware at first of what has happened. The 'model' abduction described above will be condensed to just the appearance of the UFO, the blinding light and a momentary period of confusion, then a re-awakening and the gradual realization that some minutes, hours or even days are missing from the subject's memory. Sometimes this realization will only come when the time or date is checked with another person. In a hypnotic regression session the hypnotists will talk the witness back to the time immediately before the events took place, so that he describes the surroundings and is led on to re-live his sighting. In the hypnotic state the witness will begin to describe the events that apparently took place in the missing time. Gradually, a narrative will emerge, which in most cases will be remarkably similar to our 'typical abduction'.

Before going into further general discussion of the shadowy world of the abductee, we shall look in detail at some actual cases, as they were reported in the 'ufological' magazines, in the mass-media, and in the words of the abductees themselves. Probably 80 per cent of all abduction reports have come from the USA. While there may be some social reasons for this, it is also largely due to the fact that the USA has the greatest number of active UFO researchers; has a number of nationwide media outlets that have shown themselves to be receptive to such reports; and has a well-established 'hot-line' telephone reporting service for UFO witnesses. But many other parts of the world have also originated UFO abductions: most notably South America, site of one of the first and most significant cases; Australia; Europe, and the UK.

Although there have as yet been comparatively few cases in Britain, at least by American standards, some of those which have taken place have been particularly interesting; and in common with other parts of the world, there has been a recent acceleration in the number of cases coming to public attention.

A Yorkshire encounter

UFO researchers have always been particularly impressed by accounts from policemen – for obvious reasons. Like military personnel, pilots and the like, policemen are trained observers. They are used to looking critically at events, and are perhaps less likely to panic when confronted by odd or potentially dangerous happenings. They are also known and easily identified in their community, and subject to a professional discipline.

Alan Godfrey is a constable with the West Yorkshire police force,[45] stationed in Todmorden, a small mill town in the heart of the Yorkshire wool industry. It was early in the morning of 28 November 1980, as Constable Godfrey was nearing the end of his night shift, that he drove to a local housing estate to investigate reports of stray cows invading residents' gardens. Turning into the main road he thought he saw a bus ahead of him. But he soon saw, to his alarm, that it was something the like of which he had never seen before. An object about 20 feet across was hovering about 5 feet above the roadway. It was dome-shaped, 14 feet high, with a row of darkened windows around the top half. The bottom half was spinning. He was concerned to report back to his headquarters, but found that neither the car radio, nor the personal walkie-talkie would work (a feature we find over and over again in UFO accounts of all kinds). He then decided to try to draw this strange object on one of his accident report forms – no other official stationery seemed to quite fit the circumstances – when the object suddenly disappeared.

When PC Godfrey returned to the police station he was understandably hesitant to make an official report of the incident, fearing ridicule, or at least unceasing leg-pulling from his colleagues. But when he heard that other policemen in Halifax had also seen UFOs at about the same time, he decided to report the matter fully.

After the story reached the local papers, three Manchester-based UFO investigators – Harry Harris, Mike Sachs and Norman Collinson, himself a senior police officer with the Manchester force – began a detailed investigation of the policeman's report. They started by deciding that a hypnotic regression would help fill in gaps in the constable's narrative. Although reluctant at first, he later agreed to be hypnotized by a psychiatrist who had worked with several northern police forces, using hypnotic techniques to help witnesses recall otherwise forgotten details of crimes or accidents.

Under hypnosis Alan Godfrey's conscious memory was found to be only the prologue to a remarkable series of events. While drawing the vision that confronted him, he started to get out of the car to try to get a closer look. At this moment a brilliant light shone out from the object. He jumped back into the car, and tried to drive away, but the police car would not start. Now everything went black – the fear and agitation showing in his hypnotic state (the researchers video-taped the hypnotic sessions, so all his reactions and emotions can be studied). He cries out that something is holding him. Now the light returns, and he finds himself in a room with a table. A figure is standing in front of him – a man, six feet tall, wearing a black and white robe – Godfrey describes it as a 'sheet' – and a skull-cap. He is bearded. Again, the video-recording registers the fear expressed on his face and in his voice. He shouts, 'They're horrible, horrible . . .' Now there are other creatures in the room; these newcomers are only three or four feet high, and are tugging and pulling at him. They are in no way human or humanoid; they have round faces 'like a lamp'. They seem to be communicating with each other in a strange, whistling language. The human-like figure, who Alan says is called 'Joseph', tells him that these creatures are robots, and that he is not to be frightened of them. At this point there is another, even more curious, incident. A dog enters the room. Godfrey shouts 'It's a bloody dog, it's horrible, about the size of an alsatian.'

Joseph leads him over to the table, which appears to be covered with black leather, and tries to get him to lie on it. Despite resisting at first, Godfrey suddenly decides to comply – a change of mind he is unable to explain. His hypnotic narrative continued: 'Now I'm getting onto the bed. Don't know why, I just thought I would get onto the bed. There's a light and there's Joseph, I'm lying down, there's a light . . .' At this point Godfrey began moaning, almost screaming, and displaying so much agitation that the hypnotist was forced to end the session right away.

The investigators were able to arrange another hypnotic session, this time by Robert Blair, a consultant psychiatrist and a former lecturer at Manchester University. The story revealed this time is almost identical to the first session, except that the policeman seemed to display much less emotion as he described his experiences. The second session went past the stage where Alan is lying on the bed. He describes a light above his head, and some machinery. But when he tries to look more closely at the machinery, he feels a pain in his head. He claims that he is not able to answer any questions about this machinery: 'I haven't to answer that, I haven't to tell you. Each time I think about it I get a pain.' While he was lying on the table, 'Joseph' began an examination of him: an object was placed on his arm – it felt very cold: 'It's a bit like a blood-pressure thing, it feels tingly and very cold.' Suddenly he shouted, 'There's something on my left leg,' and is astonished to discover that the robot-creatures are trying to take his shoes and socks off. Suddenly, the ordeal ends, and he is back, sitting in his police 'panda' car.

A family affair

UFO investigators in Britain had been reading the reports of abductions which were coming out of the USA, but it was not until 1974 that they had a case of their own to investigate. The case of John and Elaine Avis provided their first opportunity to undertake an in-depth analysis of an abduction report, including the use of hypnotic techniques.[12]

The Avis's names are pseudonyms, and this is now a standard practice amongst British UFO investigators who have adopted a 'code of conduct', which is intended to protect the interests of the witnesses. (PC Godfrey's case came through prior publicity in the press, so the same considerations did not apply.)

It was autumn 1974, late of an evening. John and Elaine, and their three children Kevin (10), Karen (11), and Stuart (7), were driving home from a visit to Elaine's parents through the deserted countryside on the boundaries of Essex and Greater London, towards their home in the village of Aveley. The parents sat in the front, John driving; the younger boy and the girl lay sleeping on the back seat. Kevin was looking out of the side window when he saw a light pacing the car, above some nearby houses. He pointed it out to his parents, who first thought it was an aeroplane, but as they watched it they decided that they had never seen anything like it before – oval-shaped and pale-blue in colour. It passed over the car, and then disappeared behind some trees. As they drove on they caught glimpses of it from time to time, until it was hidden by bushes. They thought the incident was over. Suddenly they began to realize that something very peculiar was happening. The sound of the car engine was no longer audible, or the sound of the tyres on the road. As they turned a bend in the road a number of things happened almost at once. They drove into a thick bank of green mist which spread right across the road; the car radio began crackling and smoking, and John pulled the wires out; the engine went dead, and the car jerked violently as the mist engulfed the vehicle. Suddenly there was a jolt, and they were driving along the road again. They continued their journey home, quiet and confused. John had the peculiar impression that when he first emerged from the mist he was alone in the front of the car.

When the couple had left Elaine's parents earlier in the evening, they were anxious to get home in time to see a television play, so one of the first things they did on arrival was to switch on the television set – to be confronted with a blank screen. They quickly switched to the other television channels, but found to their amazement that all the television stations appeared to have closed down for the night. It was only then that they thought to check the time – and received their second big shock of the night. Instead of the clock showing 10.30 in the evening, which was when they usually arrived home after the journey, it was after one o'clock in the morning. Almost three hours had vanished from their lives.

They decided to try to put these uncomfortable matters out of their minds; but they found that as time went on, disturbing reminders kept intruding. They began having dreams of strange, unearthly events and creatures; their house seemed to be invaded by a mild 'poltergeist' type of activity, which produced odd bumps, noises and tapping sounds. They began to undergo certain changes in their lifestyle. John had a nervous breakdown and lost his job.

These events and memories became a preoccupation, so that when John read a newspaper article and listened to a local radio programme on UFOs he decided to contact a UFO research group. Soon after, the family were contacted by Andrew Collins, an Essex-based UFO investigator, and his colleagues. They soon decided that the Avis family were reasonable, sincere people whose story deserved to be taken seriously. They also decided that the mystery of the missing hours should be investigated by hypnosis.

We now have two cases where regression techniques have been employed, and it is worth looking a little more closely at what this involves. Regression hypnosis has been used by UFO investigators since the famous 'Hill Case' of 1961 – the details of this case will be summarized briefly in another chapter. It presented the first case in which details of a period of 'missing time' in a UFO close encounter case were brought out through the use of hypnotism, and revealed an abduction scenario. Hypnotic regression is a controversial subject, the very nature of which is important to any consideration of the abduction phenomenon. Basically, hypnosis simply relaxes the subject, freeing his or her mind from any distractions and allowing them to concentrate unreservedly on whatever topic they are directed to by the hypnotist. Memories and details which have hitherto been forgotten can be unearthed by this procedure. But there is a danger, too, that 'confabulation' might take place. This is the creation of false 'memories', and may result in the subject coming up with whatever they think the hypnotist may want to hear. To avoid this, a skilled practitioner will try to avoid all questions which might, however accidentally, lead the subject towards a particular answer. It has been a source of controversy in more than one hypnotic regression case as to whether or not the technique and questioning of the practitioner was prejudging the percipient's story as it was emerging.

Nevertheless, in the Avis case (which tends to be called the 'Aveley Abduction' in the UFO literature, after the village near where the family's adventures took place) the investigators decided to go ahead with a hypnotic regression, under the direction of Dr Leonard Wilder, a dentist. John was willing to undergo regression but his wife refused, wishing to put the events behind her (a curious pattern which recurs in several other cases, as we shall see). In a series of three sessions, a remarkable story emerged. Other details came from conscious recollections after the hypnotic sessions had finished.

John's first recollection inside the UFO was of standing on a 'balcony' looking down into a giant, hangar-like room. Below he could see a car with occupants, two people in the front seats, more in the back, all asleep or slumped over the seats. On the balcony he found he was standing next to Elaine, and behind him was a tall figure, well over six feet high. John and this 'person' walk through a door, which suddenly appears in an otherwise blank wall. They pass along a corridor and enter an 'examination room', furnished with a table and various apparatus. The tall entity touches him, and he blacks out.

When he recovered his senses, he found himself lying on the table, surrounded by the apparatus, part of which was moving up and down over his body. Three of the tall entities stood watching while this was going on, but to his left he caught sight of two other figures, who seemed to be examining him with small, pen-like instruments. Unlike the tall humanoid individuals, these were grotesque, alien things. They had triangular eyes, a beaked nose and slit-mouth. Their ears were huge and pointed, their hands hairy and clawlike. But what made them even more hideous, if that were possible, was that they were wearing what looked like white surgical gowns. The taller creatures were more human looking. They wore a silvery, one-piece suit, which also covered their head, and possibly their mouths and noses (John could not recall seeing these features).

After the examination was completed the humanoids explained the function of their instruments, including a kind of mask which enabled them to see clearly whilst on Earth. Then John was taken down more passageways, and was shown various parts of the craft – a 'rest and recreation' area, which contained sleeping cubicles – and then into a control room.

In this room John was made to lie down, and a series of images appeared above his head on a dish-shaped 'screen'. These included pictures of plans, drawings and charts which flashed past too quickly for him to get a clear view of them. A few of the things he can recall are diagrams of the solar system, and views of the planet Saturn. At the same time there was a verbal 'commentary'. Next he was taken to a three-dimensional 'holographic' image. It showed a scene of grey, metallic cones, under a lurid coloured sky. It was explained to him that this is what the Earth will look like after it has been destroyed by pollution. Standing in front of this scene appeared a robed figure who held out a round glowing sphere, which

John was asked to touch, whereupon he felt a strange sensation in his arm. He had the idea that this hologram represented some kind of a 'shrine' for the tall beings.

Now a figure whom he had identified as the leader of the humanoids told him that it was time to leave, and just a few moments later he found himself back in the car, but a few hundred yards along the road from the last point he could remember.

The 'Examiners' and 'Controllers' described in the Avis abduction experience.

Elaine's conscious memories of her experience are broadly similar to her husband's. She can recall being with him on the balcony, but says that their elder son Kevin was with them too. She also looked down and saw a car in the 'hangar', but this time it was definitely their car – because she could see John and Kevin standing by it *also*! Then she was led away, and Kevin was taken away from her. She found herself in an examination room like the one John was led to but with two tables. She was put on one of them, strapped down by her hands and ankles, and given an examination similar to John's, with the small grotesque creatures going over her body with the 'pens'. When she eventually got down from the table she found that she was wearing a long gown with a hood, although she has no recollection of getting undressed or of putting it on. She was led away through more corridors (catching sight of John on one occasion, who seemed to take no notice of her), and then into the control room. Like John, she was shown a series of images on a screen. One of them seems to have been a 'zoom' shot on a cosmic scale. At first she saw stars in space, and was told that this represented 'Home'. Gradually the field of view concentrated on one star, moving closer and closer until she could make out the outline of the British Isles, then the Thames Estuary, individual towns, buildings, streets and houses, until she was again told that this is where she lives. Another screen then flashed a series of images such as John had been shown; she reported that it was 'like having the contents of an encyclopaedia pumped into one's head all in one go'. Next came the 'hologram', and she too was told to touch the luminous sphere held by the robed figure. She was told 'This is the seed of life, our past and your future, our whole existence. Accept this from us for yourselves, your children and your fellow kind.'

After these messages she was led back to the car, which was resting on a ramp in a kind of stepped amphitheatre. The children were already in the car, and John was standing by the door, about to get in. Suddenly the car vanished before her eyes, as if through the wall of the craft. Elaine became alarmed, but was told not to worry. Then she became aware of seeing the car moving along the lane, and of herself getting into it as it was still moving.

With a sudden jolt the experience was over, and she was in the car sitting next to her husband.

The soldier and the little bearded men

Both of these cases seem to provide supporting evidence for the theory, held by many, probably a majority, of UFO investigators that the abductions are part of a programme of investigation by some alien race surveying our planet and examining its flora and fauna – including *homo sapiens*. The human specimens they gather are examined in laboratory conditions by means of advanced technology instruments. From time to time the humans are given some insight into the background and methods of their abductors, and concern is expressed at the present direction of human society on Earth. It is interesting that in these cases, as in many others, there appear to be two types of creatures involved – a smaller, non-human or robotic entity, usually more than one, and a larger, more human, or even totally human figure, who appears to be in overall control of the operations.

But there are some cases where this pattern does not seem to hold, and the activities of the alien abductors do not seem to correspond with the methods of scientific investigation.

José Antonio da Silva was a respected member of the Brazilian Armed Forces, orderly to a Deputy Commander of the Military Police. On the evening of 3 May 1969 he had taken some time out to do a spot of fishing near a place called Bebedouro, about 50km from the City of Belo Horizonte, where he lived. He set up camp on the banks of a small lake and settled down for the night. Throughout the next day, Sunday, he sat fishing, but the fish were not biting. About three o'clock in the afternoon he heard voices and saw figures moving behind him, but did not take too much notice, thinking that it was other campers. Suddenly one of the newcomers uttered a harsh, rasping groan, and da Silva felt his legs being burned by a blast of fire which came from a weapon the figure was holding.[1]

He saw now that these people were not campers, but two stockily built masked figures, who seized him by his arms and dragged him off across the swampy ground. They passed another of the creatures, who followed them. His captors were a little over four feet high, of human proportions, their heads covered by metallic helmets, with eye-holes and what looked like a breathing apparatus running from the front of the helmet to a container on their back.

Eventually they reached a 'craft', a rather odd machine, which does not seem to feature in other abduction reports. Da Silva later described it by placing a tumbler upright on a saucer, and placing another saucer on top, upside-down like a lid. Slanting tubes ran from the rim of the top 'saucer' into the bottom of the 'tumbler'. The whole apparatus was about six feet high and eight feet in diameter. Antonio and the two creatures who held him entered the contraption through a small door in the side, and he found himself in a compartment with walls which seemed to be composed of a stone-like material. The lighting was like a sodium light, but came from no visible source. A sort of bench ran along one of the walls, and the captors pushed da Silva down onto it. Then they forced a helmet onto his head, like the ones they wore. It was an uncomfortable fit, and pressed against his shoulders. He was fastened into the seat, and the two creatures made themselves secure as well. Da Silva could now only see what was going on through the limited vision afforded by the eye-holes.

Now the third of the aliens entered, sat down, and then moved a small lever on the floor. Immediately there was a humming sound, and the sensation of movement.

The uncomfortable ride appeared to go on for hours, during which the compartment seemed to change direction more than once. The light began to pulsate brilliantly, until there was a jolt, and the movement seemed to stop. The creatures unfastened themselves from the seats, released the soldier, then, covering the holes in his helmet so that he could not see, led him out of the compartment. He could hear footsteps and the sound of many voices. Eventually he was made to sit again, still with the helmet on. But now he could see the beings without their 'space-suits'.

They were dwarfish and stocky, with very long beards and hair which fell down below their waists. Their faces had big noses, very bushy eyebrows, big ears and apparently toothless mouths. Da Silva identified one of the creatures as being in command of the others, who clustered around him. Although his view was still restricted by the helmet, as he tried to move his head he could make out features of the room. This, too, appeared to be made of stone, and the illumination had the same 'sourceless' quality as in the craft. One of the walls bore pictures of earthly scenes - houses, building, vehicles, animals (including a giraffe) and other scenes.

But what he saw on a wide shelf beneath these figures filled him with terror. Lying side by side on their backs were the dead, naked bodies of four men. The bodies seemed quite human, one was black, another dark-skinned.

The small creatures began to search through the bundle of belongings he had hung onto all through this ordeal. Excitedly they began checking the items of food, fishing tackle, money and identity cards he had brought with him. They took away one example of everything for which there was a duplicate, but also took his identity card. The dwarfs were jabbering and gesticulating as they examined each article. At one point one of them fired a weapon of the type which had burned da Silva's leg. It made a burn mark on the wall which bore the pictures.

The being da Silva had identified as the 'Chief' approached him and attempted to communicate by means of gestures and symbols drawn on a greyish tablet. The drawings seemed to consist of concentric circles, which Antonio took to represent days and years. He concluded that the message was a proposition: he should stay on Earth for three more years, observing and spying for the aliens; then he would go with them for seven years, to study their ways. After the ten years were up they would land on Earth with him as their guide. He gestured his refusal of this offer. Perhaps fearing his fate – were those the bodies of others who has refused? – he began to finger a Rosary which he wore like a belt around his waist. The 'Chief' snatched the Rosary away from him, spilling its beads all over the floor, to the interest of the other onlookers.

Suddenly a figure appeared before Antonio, materializing apparently from nowhere. It was invisible to the small beings, who took no notice of it, and continuing talking amongst themselves. The figure was of a man, totally human, of average size, wearing a long, monk-like robe. He spoke in fluent Portuguese, and gave Antonio a message which he said should not be passed on for several years. Da Silva, when interviewed by investigators, was very reticent, not only about this message, but even about the man's physical description, claiming that the details of his revelation could be deduced just from a description of the person. The figure vanished as suddenly as it had appeared, and as he did so the dwarfs began squabbling with each other. The 'Chief' again approached the captive, and more hands covered the eye-holes in the helmet. He was led off to the cylindrical craft, and the long journey began again. Eventually, he felt the jolt that announced arrival, the helmet was pulled off, and he was dragged out of the small craft into the open air. He lay, semi-conscious, sprawled on the ground for about an hour. When he had fully recovered his senses, he drank deeply from a nearby stream, and caught a fish which he cooked and ate. He stumbled onwards and eventually found a road, where he was able to ask directions from other travellers. To his astonishment he found that he was near the city of Victoria, nearly two hundred miles from Bebedouro and his home in Belo Horizonte. More astonishingly, it was over four days from the time that his ordeal had begun.

Tired, hungry, his leg hurting where it had been struck by the beam from the aliens' weapon, his neck and shoulders raw from the pressure and rubbing of the helmet, he eventually stumbled into a small country railway station. Here he blurted out his story to a railway official, who took him home, where he was fed and rested. Eventually, with the money which had been returned to him by his captors, he returned to Belo Horizonte, and told his story to senior officers at his barracks. Within the week this remarkable abduction was being investigated by a team of people from the Brazilian UFO research group CICOANI.

This story differs in many important ways from the accounts of the Avis family and PC Godfrey, but it also has many similarities. Although it runs in the familiar pattern of capture, examination, two kinds of creatures, message and release, there is little in the narrative which puts it into a specifically 'extraterrestrial' context – apart from the cylindrical 'craft' into which he was first led. The interior in which he was held had none of the space-age trappings of control consoles, screens, high-technology medicals laboratories, etc. The walls of both the small craft and the large room were reported as being constructed of stone, which makes little sense for the design of a spaceship, and is more suggestive of underground than outer space. Even the furniture and a small cubic cup he drank a green liquid from were made of stone. The beards of his captors seem particularly incongruous; one can hardly imagine such hirsute creatures being very comfortable in spacesuits. In fact, apart from the initial capture, this whole encounter seems to have more in common with fairy-tales of dwarfs and gnomes than with the activities of aliens from space. The mysterious robed figure (which appears, significantly, just after his Rosary is torn off him) seems to have more in common with religious apparitions of Christ or the saints, than with anyone who might reasonably be thought to have business aboard an interplanetary space craft.

All these facets of the Bebedouro abduction have great significance for the phenomenon as a whole, as we shall see in the next chapter.

TWO: THE HISTORICAL PERSPECTIVE

UFO abductions, the apparent kidnapping of human beings by UFO entities, is by and large a phenomenon of the past ten years or so. But for a long time before then people have been claiming that they have been taken aboard flying saucers. The difference in these cases is that for the most part the visit to the alien craft was voluntary.

Many of these claims originated in America in the early and mid-fifties, and amongst those people who were beginning to take an interest in the UFO mystery the people involved became known as the 'contactees' – because they claimed contact with the beings in control of the saucers. At the time, and for a decade afterwards, the contactees were seen by many UFO researchers as a major embarrassment. In the 1950s, UFO research was conducted in a quasi-military atmosphere. It was the stated aim of the largest American UFO research group, NICAP (National Investigation Committee on Aerial Phenomena), to present evidence to the American political and military Establishment that they hoped would prove the reality of the UFOs as vehicles of alien visitors. The evidence they sought was based largely on reliable eyewitness testimony by such people as pilots, police officers, community leaders, scientists, and other similar figures whose testimony NICAP thought would be most acceptable to the government and the armed forces. Throughout the fifties NICAP and similar organizations compiled impressive dossiers of sighting reports, with analyses by astronomers and other scientists sympathetic to their aims. Amid all this painstaking work the presence of a small number of people who claimed to be meeting the occupants of the saucers on an almost daily basis, talking to them and riding in their craft, was an irritant that the scientific groups felt would undermine their own efforts to be taken seriously by Establishment science.[25, 34]

As a result, the contactees were shunned by most of the bigger groups; consequently, their influence was strongest amongst the many newly emerging groups that saw the coming of the UFOs in an almost religious light. In fact many of these groups evolved from fringe sects and cults, and quickly adopted the growing UFO lore as part of their articles of faith. The cultists eagerly accepted the contactees' stories at face value. To the dismay of the 'respectable' researchers, the cults became a dominant part of the public's image of the UFO mystery.

Best known of all the contactees was George Adamski, a complex figure who is still a centre of controversy today, fifteen years after his death and over twenty-five years after the first of his alleged contacts. Adamski's encounters took place in the Californian desert, near the world-famous Mount Palomar Observatory. Here he would be met by classic domed saucers piloted by tall, long-haired, beautiful, human-like creatures who took him aboard their craft. Between flying him to the Moon, Mars and other planets, they offered him words of warning and advice for him to spread to the rest of mankind – which he did. In a series of books and worldwide lecture tours he took the Venusians' messages across the globe. In later years he would tell of his meetings with Pope Pius XII (disputed by others), Queen Juliana of the Netherlands (indisputable) and other prominent political and social figures. By the time of his death he was a hero to one part of the ufological fraternity, but a figure of distrust and derision to the other.[37, 53]

His stories of meetings with extraterrestrials, and the photographs which he produced in evidence, were denounced as a crude hoax. His most famous photograph was alleged to be everything from a chicken feeder to a lampshade with three ping-pong balls. This produced a curious postscript in 1977 when a UFO researcher in London announced in the press that when he was sitting in a Covent Garden restaurant he noticed that the restaurant's bottle-cooler bore a most remarkable resemblance to Adamski's UFO. Here, he proclaimed, was the final solution. The discovery caused a minor uproar in the UFO world, with pro- and anti-Adamski factions denouncing each other. The matter was settled to no one's particular satisfaction when the designer of the bottle-cooler appeared, to announce that, as a UFO buff himself, he had actually based *his* design on Adamski's photograph!

But George Adamski, although the best known of the contactees, was by no means the only one, and not the most typical. Throughout the 1950s, and beyond, a stream of books by different contactees served only to cloud the UFO scene – each writer having a rather different tale to tell. However, common threads ran through almost all these claims. None of the contactees were 'abducted' in the way described in the last chapter. The human-like beings they met seemed friendly, kind and wise; they brought only help and inspiration, warning or advice. Often they claimed to be representatives of an interplanetary 'parliament' or 'council' that maintained a watching brief over the somewhat primitive inhabitants of planet Earth. Cases of contacts like this have continued until the present day – we can see elements in the Aveley case, amongst others; but gradually another type of contact began to emerge, one that was more acceptable to the serious scientific ufologist.

In the late 1950s and early 1960s reports began to come in of people claiming contact with a different type of UFO occupant: beings with a less human appearance, and without the quasi-religious overtones of the 'Venusian Space-brothers'. Witnesses now began to tell of meetings with small, rather grotesque creatures. Far from attempting to contact the witness, these entities were more likely to ignore him or even flee from him. The first major outbreak of these reports came from France during a great wave of UFO sightings that swept the country in 1954.[42] Here, and in later cases throughout the world, the witnesses would typically see a grounded saucer attended by two or three small figures, 2½ to 3½ feet high, with disproportionately large heads and hands, large eyes and some sort of back-pack or breathing apparatus. These creatures would perhaps be collecting samples of earth or plants, or carrying out repairs to their craft. This strangeness of appearance, such as one might expect of creatures from an alien environment, coupled with a fairly reasonable sort of behaviour, made these new reports more acceptable to many ufologists who had previously been scornful of the 'space-brother' contactees. Even so, many of the hard-liners seemed to find a UFO quite acceptable if it was flying around a few hundred feet above the ground, with its pilots shrouded in a decent obscurity; but it was quite beyond the pale if the UFO dared to land and its occupants get out to stretch their legs – an anomalous position, which owed more to 'gut-feeling' than logic.

Although most of these reports indicated that the 'occupants' were indifferent to or wary of humans, there was a steady undercurrent to some of the reports which suggested an element of hostility. This caused some reports to be hushed up by researchers who had been emotionally committed to the idea of a benevolent extraterrestrial intelligence. Many people felt that if the UFOs were craft from a more advanced civilization elswhere in the galaxy, then that civilization must of necessity be a peaceful one. A not illogical view, but one which was not borne out by some of the reports that passed through ufologists' hands.

Numerous stories of hostility by the saucer occupants came from South America. On the evening of 16 December 1954, three young men were driving from the town of San Carlos, Venezuela. One, who ventured away from the car when they stopped for a while, claimed to have been set upon by a small, hairy-looking creature, which ran off to a flat, shiny object hovering above the ground, which then rose into the sky. The man who was attacked, Jesus Paz, was rushed off to hospital and treated for several deep scratches along his body. Police investigating the incident found extensive signs of a struggle by the roadside.[6]

As the contactee phenomenon began to be superseded by the more 'alien' type of encounter, there was also a geographical widening of the area where the reports arose. The contactee cases had been limited almost entirely to the USA, whereas the second wave of entity reports began in France. spreading rapidly to other parts of Europe and to North and South America.

It was in South America that some of the most sensational contacts took place. Throughout the 1950s and 1960s a stream of reports came from Brazil, Argentina, Venezuela and the other countries of the continent. Some of the stories appearing in the UFO magazines were little more than rumours, reprinted from obscure local papers or sensationalist tabloids, without any sort of corroboration or first-hand investigation. Thus we are presented with bizarre stories such as that of a UFO parked at the side of a street in Caracas, Venezuela, for several hours, while its 'occupants' floated in and out through the walls of a neighbouring apartment block!

Fortunately, not all the reports emanating from South America were of such a flimsy nature. Many had been investigated in depth by small groups of respected investigators who were trying to make some sort of sense out of the hundreds of reports that bombarded them. Dr Olavo Fontes of Brazil was one such investigator, and his report on one of the first UFO abduction cases has become something of a classic. News of the case was first broken to English speaking readers in a series of articles in the leading British UFO magazine *Flying Saucer Review* under the title of 'The Most Amazing Case of All' – a title which seemed no exaggeration when the full story was out.[10]

Waves of intense activity swept the South American states throughout the 1950s and 1960s. In 1957 much of the activity centred on Brazil; so much so that the coastal regions of that country from Rio de Janeiro to Sao Paulo became known to UFO enthusiasts as 'Saucer Alley'.

Further to the south, in Minas Gerais province, the weather was so hot in the southern hemisphere spring that two young farmers found it easier to do their ploughing at night. It was at 11 p.m. on the night of 14 October that Antonio Villas Boas and his brother saw a light in the sky that moved about and seemed to follow them across the fields. Eventually this persistent activity scared them so much that they gave up work for the night. The following night Antonio was out working alone when the light made its reappearance. It rushed towards him, then halted about 300 feet above the fields. Again he uncoupled the ploughing gear and started to drive for home. But this time he was terrified to find that his tractor would not start. Suddenly the light in the sky swooped down and landed just a few yards away from him. Two figures emerged from the 'craft', running after him as he fled and eventually grabbing his arms. Despite his desperate struggles he was hauled into the craft, a disc-shaped object with a rim and fins protruding from it. He found himself in a circular compartment furnished with a three-legged table and a shaft or pillar in the middle, from floor to ceiling. Rubber tubes were attached to his chin, apparently to draw blood from him. Next he was stripped and conducted to another compartment, which contained a white, plastic-like couch. The creatures that had captured him were dressed in tight-fitting metallic suits with round helmets which had narrow visors through which their faces could not be seen. They laid him down on the couch and proceeded to wash him with a kind of sponge containing a refreshing liquid. A sudden pungent smell caused Villas Boas to be violently sick.

A door opened and another figure approached him – not, this time, one of the space-suited entities, but a totally human-looking, and rather beautiful, blonde woman. She was about 4′ 8″ tall, with small, finely detailed features, slanted oriental-looking eyes, and high cheekbones. But what astonished the witness even more was that she was completely naked.

A rather embarrassed Antonio Villas Boas admitted later to Dr Fontes that he had quite enjoyed the act of sex that followed. So, it would appear, did the woman, as 'after more caresses' they repeated it. He was, though, disturbed by the strange, guttural barks the woman made, similar to the sounds he had heard from his original captors. After she left, one of the other creatures returned with his clothes, leaving him to dress himself and return to the room where he had first been taken. Here three of the crew were sitting talking, and he had time to observe his surroundings. One thing which caught his attention was a square box with a clock-like dial on one face. It had marks for the 'quarter-hours', but just one hand, which did not move in all the time he watched it. He attempted to remove this device, but one of his captors snatched it from him angrily. Eventually he was released and returned home. His story only emerged several years later, when local researchers began hearing rumours that the Brazilian secret service had started to take an interest in an alleged local UFO case.

Many of the ufologists who interested themselves in the case felt that this was an incident involving selective breeding, a bringing-together of human beings and the space people for the purpose of creating a new interplanetary super-race. It is certainly an interpretation which fits the story as reported by Villas Boas. One British writer even asked if the ultimate aim was to 'breed a new race . . . who are destined to live here, and to populate the vast, uninhabited areas of Brazil . . .?'

The idea of the deliberate inter-breeding of human beings with some sort of superior extraterrestrial civilization is one which many students of ufology have found particularly interesting. It has been put forward by such writers as Erich von Däniken, but was being discussed earlier, in the 1950s by the English ufologist Brinsley le Poer Trench (now Lord Clancarty), in a series of books which introduced many of the ideas subsequently taken up by the protagonists of the 'ancient astronauts' theory. These writers have usually gone as far back as Biblical references to giants coupling with the daughters of men as precedents for UFO abductions with a sexual overtone.

But there are many objections, on a purely biological level, to such a literal explanation of Antonio Villas Boas's experience. It seems impossible that two races of creatures, presumably evolving through completely different biological systems on planets probably millions of light years apart, should have sufficient genetic relationship to allow such interbreeding to take place. Even in the report that Villas Boas gives us there are a number of unanswered questions that preclude a simple extraterrestrial explanation. Why, for instance, did the beings who hauled him onto the saucer wear helmets and apparently elaborate breathing apparatus, even on board the ship, whilst the woman appeared naked? Were they perhaps of two different races? Yet they both spoke in the same inhuman manner, so their vocal chords must have been similar – which would have been unlikely if they had both developed in differently constituted atmospheres.

Through the subsequent years the number of abduction reports has increased steadily, and the character of them seems to have changed. Apart from the extraordinarily personal nature of Villas Boas's experience, many of the first reports were quite impersonal. They seemed to reflect the objective type of 'scientific investigation' that appeared to preoccupy the entities involved in other UFO contact cases of the period. The most famous of the early abductions is the Hill case, which happened in the

White Mountains of New England in 1961. This case has been the subject of at least one full length book, and has featured in numerous magazine articles as well as in almost every UFO book covering that period. There is little point in dwelling on the details of it in any great depth, except to state that after a mysterious 'time loss' experience following a UFO sighting whilst the couple were driving through New Hampshire on their way back from a holiday in Canada, the Hills were regressed hypnotically to the time of their sighting. In separate sessions conducted by the Boston psychiatrist Dr Benjamin Simon they each told of being taken aboard a UFO by strange oriental-eyed beings, who subjected them to an impersonal medical examination. Two curious features of this perhaps reflect the sexual overtones of the Villas Boas case. At one point Betty claimed that a long, needle-like object was inserted into her abdomen, through her navel, and this has been regarded by some researchers as a kind of pregnancy test. Barney reported a cup-like instrument which was placed over his genitals, and subsequently a ring of small warts developed where it had been placed. Again, this has been interpreted as some kind of sperm-test, or a collection of semen for artificial insemination.[23]

Throughout their abduction the Hills felt that their treatment was quite detached, that they were being treated like animals in a laboratory, of interest only for their reactions.

Cases like these added to the growing conviction amongst most students of the UFO phenomenon that the abductions were part of a logical pattern of behaviour on the part of the UFO entities. Earth, they said, was under investigation. Our scientists were setting out for the moon, where they would gather samples of rocks and minerals; in the remote possibility of any life-forms beings found, they would be examined too. Were not the ufonauts conducting a similar experimental investigation of earth? They were landing in sparsely populated parts of the world, where they would be seen, if at all, by a few isolated and remote people. Here they gathered samples of rocks and plants, used strange instruments to measure things, and from time to time they would investigate the many life forms that populate this planet.

Occasionally this would mean taking human beings into laboratories on their craft and subjecting them to detailed examination. The entities who examined Betty and Barney must have only just started their investigation of *homo sapiens* – they seemed fascinated by Barney's false teeth, and tried to pull out Betty's own set, fortunately without success! So that their guinea-pigs would not remember their experience, they were apparently subjected to a post-hypnotic suggestion that they would remember nothing of their ordeal. This was certainly a logical and coherent scenario. It presumed little more than an extension of the technology and motivation we ourselves were demonstrating. If there were any inconsistencies revealed by investigation of the reported cases, this was probably due more to our lack of understanding of the working methods of the aliens than to any internal contradiction in the *modus operandi* of our visitors.

In the years following the Villas Boas and Hill cases to the present day, the abduction scenario has become established as a central feature of the UFO phenomenon. Researchers who dismissed the 'space brothers' of Adamski as the result of a wistful yearning for a secure universe, in which man's folly might be tempered by benign extraterrestrial intervention, were more prepared to accept the coldly rational manner of the agents behind the abductions. It would seem in the most recent cases, however, a trend can be observed towards a more 'interventionist' approach by the UFO denizens. Abductees like the Aveley couple (Chapter One) tell of warnings of imminent disaster, through nuclear or environmental misuse. It is hard to know at this stage if this is an objective change in the nature of the abduction phenomenon itself, or whether it reflects the re-emerging concern in recent years about the danger of nuclear war or some other form of planetary holocaust. We are, after all, less than two decades away from the end of a millenium, an epoch which has traditionally been associated with apocalyptic preoccupations.

Abductions on the Celtic fringe

So far we have been looking at the abduction report solely in a ufological context. But there is no clear dividing line between this and a number of other areas of human experience in which we come across reports of humans being abducted by strange or unearthly creatures. One of the main storehouses of such tales is the vast number of bizarre and weird stories which constitute the folk and fairy lore of many lands. Although these legends have now been consigned to the decorative fringes of our society, in the past they formed part of the accepted knowledge and world-view of the great proportion of the population. Although fairy stories are now dressed up in the effete literary garb of the eighteenth century, or firmly catalogued and dissected by rationalist, nineteenth-century collectors, their origins are in the everyday experiences of the common people throughout history. Pushed into the shadows by the growth of religious and state-controlled education and the rise of science, the fairy faiths of Europe lasted into the twentieth century on the rocky fringes of Europe, in the Celtic nations of Scotland, Ireland, Wales, Cornwall, the Isle of Man, and Britanny. In the stories from these lands we find many reports that uncannily parallel the abduction experience.

Much of our knowledge of these stories comes from the painstaking work of a small number of dedicated researchers who scoured the remote parts of Europe in the early years of this century, speaking to the old people about what had been told to them by their parents, about what they remembered from their youth, and, in the farthest and remotest parts, about what was still reputed to be happening in the fields and mountains around them.

The motives of these folklorists were varied. Some like Lady Gregory of Coole, patroness of W. B. Yeats, were seeking inspiration for a romantic, nationalist revival. Others were seeking their own origins in the Celtic past, others were inspired by the pure light of scientific enquiry. And the motives of those who gave them information were similarly mixed. Some may have been trying to preserve some of the magic they knew of in their youth, others shared the fervour of the researchers. But doubtless others were just after the price of a drink, or eager to please these strange visitors from distant cities by telling them the tales they wanted to hear, and probably from time to time making them just that wee bit more exciting! But whatever the storytellers' motives, their tales still came from that great oral library which had grown up over the centuries in these remote communities.

The legends, the lore, and even the day-to-day gossip of these people revealed a thread of stories in which men and women are taken from their normal world, and live for a few hours, days, weeks, even years, in a weird and magical other world. Consider this case, taken from the writings of J. Evans-Wentz, who travelled the Celtic countries at the turn of the century gathering word-of-mouth evidence for his classic work *The Fairy Faith in Celtic Countries*. The speaker is a ninety-two-year-old man who is recalling a tale told to him eighty years before by his grandfather:

> A boy ten years old was often whipped and cruelly treated by his schoolmaster because he could not say his lessons . . . So one day he ran away from school and went to a river-side where some little folk came down to him and asked why he was crying. He told them . . . and on hearing this they said, 'Oh! if you stay with us it will not be necessary for you to go to school, we will keep you as long as you like.'[11]

The boy is taken into a cave and enters a great palace in which other children are dancing and playing games.

Eventually the boy decides he wants to return to his mother and to take her a golden ball which the *tylwyth teg* (the fairies) have given him. But when he comes to leave, the ball is taken from him and he is pushed into the river, whence he finds his way home. The old man's story concludes:

He told his mother how he had been away a fortnight as he thought, but she told him it had been for two years. Though the boy often tried to find the way back to the *tylwyth teg* he never could. Finally he went back to school and became a most wonderful scholar and parson.

Another folklorist from the turn of the century, Edwin Hartland, reports this story, also from Wales, in his book *The Science of Fairy Tales*. A young boy has disappeared:

During the whole two years nothing was heard of him, but at length one morning when his mother, who had long and bitterly mourned him for dead, opened the door, whom should she see but Gitto, with a bundle under his arm. He was dressed and looked exactly as when she had last seen him, for he had not grown a bit. 'Where have you been all this time?' asked his mother. 'Why, it was only yesterday I went away,' he replied, and opening the bundle he showed her a dress the 'little children' as he called them, had given him for dancing with them. The dress was made of paper without a seam.[26]

Hartland concludes his account: 'With maternal caution she put it on the fire'. The modern ufologist could only deplore this destruction of what might have been a vital piece of physical evidence!

Although most of the stories collected by people like Wentz, Hartland and Lady Gregory were traditional tales of happenings many years previously, or adventures which had happened to the customary 'friend of a friend', some were first-hand narratives. For instance, this story from a Mr T. C. Kermode, a member of the Manx House

The abduction of children, and their replacement by a fairy child, was a very real fear in many country areas in Europe in the past. Illustration by E. Gertrude Thomson (1886).

of Keys (Parliament), who told Wentz of his own experience:

About forty years ago, I and another young man were . . . walking along, talking. My friend happened to look across the river and said 'Oh, look, there are the fairies. Did you ever see them?' I looked across the river and saw a circle of supernatural light . . . and into this circle of light, from the surrounding sides apparently, I saw come in twos and threes a great number of little beings.

Kermode's friends seemed more interested in the party

they were on their way to than in investigating this phenomenon any further. When Kermode struck the wall at the side of the lane with his stick, the vision vanished. It is easy to see how an experience like this – a strange circular light attended by numerous small humanoids – could so easily be interpreted, in a different climate of opinion, as a UFO close encounter sighting.

Even in the nineteenth century the traditional ways of life in the Celtic fringe were dying out. Except perhaps in the far West of Ireland, or in the remotest islands of Scotland, the influence of the modern world, and the Anglicization of the Celtic culture, were already signalling the end of the Fairy Faiths the folklorists chronicled. Most of the witnesses who gave their testimony were in their seventies and eighties, and were often reporting what their parents and grandparents had told them. But throughout the reported experiences of those who claimed to have been 'taken' by the fairies, we can see a number of factors that eerily parallel features that reappear hundreds of years later in the UFO abduction reports.

Perhaps the most significant parallel between both sets of reports is the 'time warp' factor, by which time itself appears to be manipulated so that a few hours in the fairy realm (or the UFO) become days in the world outside; a week in fairyland can be half a lifetime in daylight reality. We have already seen how the victims of UFO abductions seem to have 'missing time' – sometimes they have no memories of several hours of their lives. Often, even when hypnotic regression techniques have filled out some of the missing hours, there are still major inconsistencies between the time the abductees experienced during their abduction, and the time that was passing outside their strange environment.

In *The Science of Fairytales*, first published in 1890, Edwin Hartland devotes several chapters to what he called 'the supernatural lapse of time' in fairyland. Casting his net wider than the Celtic lands, Hartland collected tales from all over Europe and beyond, including this odd

Tales of 'fairy dances' and encounters with the 'little people' have survived into the twentieth century in the remoter parts of Europe. A seventeenth-century woodcut.

one from legend-haunted Transylvania. A student at Kronstadt (Brasov) was wandering in the mountains, rehearsing a sermon he was to preach the following Sunday. Suddenly he saw a beautiful bird and while trying to catch it he was led into a cavern. Here he met a dwarf, and was shown a great treasure. Eventually he escaped into the fresh air – to find that a century had elapsed since he had disappeared – causing great problems when he had failed to turn up at the church! At the conclusion of the tale Hartland reports:

The student was hungry with his hundred year fast, and he sat down with the others at the common table to dine. But he had no sooner eaten the first spoonful of soup than his whole frame underwent a change. From a ruddy youth he became an old man in the last stages of decrepitude.

Although we have no records of similarly dramatic fates overtaking UFO abductees on their return, we are reminded of John Avis, the Aveley abductee:

Overnight, all but the youngest child Stuart, found they could no longer face the sight of animal flesh; cooked or uncooked. It absolutely repulsed them. Elaine felt she could no longer go near a butcher's shop and John felt he was about to be sick every time he smelt the, to him, foul odour of meat cooking.[13]

Another feature of fairylore which has a curious parallel in the UFO abduction evidence is the curious way that any object brought back from fairyland – 'physical evidence' the ufologists would call it – has a strange, equivocal nature. Like the paper dress given to little Gitto, or armsful of treasure given to other visitors to fairyland, the gifts seem worthless in the real world – the evidence is destroyed in fear, or the treasure turns into a pile of golden autumn leaves. There is a most remarkable modern parallel to this in an abduction case recorded in one of the world's more obscure publications, the *Malaysian UFO Bulletin*. In January 1982 a certain Abdul Mutalib, an eighteen-year-old soldier, was found to be missing from his post guarding the rifle-range of a recruit training centre at Port Dickson, about thirty miles from Kuala-Lumpur. The Centre launched a search, without success:

According to the Centre's sources, such disappearances have occurred several times in the past, but the victims have usually returned after several days. They are believed to have been abducted by elemental beings known in Malaysia as the *Buni* people. On their return the abductees report that they went to a distant place and were given delicious food. When they vomited it was found to consist of worms and grasses.[39]

There are still some remote and secret parts of the Celtic world where it seems that the old legends still live. Whilst carrying out the research for this book, I was told by someone who had worked on the west coast of Ireland in the 1960s of an incident recounted to him by the schoolmaster of the County Donegal village of Teelin. He told how a seven-year-old girl had gone missing from the village for three days. Despite incessant heavy rain, when the child reappeared at her parents' doorstep she was quite dry. Villagers were convinced that she had been abducted into the fairy 'rath' or mound, a feature, often well hidden, of many Irish villages. Despite the encroachments of the modern world, the Celtic fairyland, it would seem, is not yet quite dead.

Supernatural abductions in the twentieth century

From the haunted coasts of Europe in the nineteenth century, we cross the Atlantic to the equally magic-ridden land of Haiti, where the abduction stories begin to take on a modern and oddly familiar appearance.

The people of Haiti still live, for the most part, in fear of the sorcerers, the *zobop*, who have occult power over all aspects of their lives through the terrifying *voodoo* cult. Haiti is perhaps the nearest approach in the world today to the superstition- and magic-dominated societies of the middle ages, but made all the more disturbing when fitted with the trappings of the twentieth century. The *zobops* are semi-mythical figures who commit the most hideous and bloody acts and who abduct people to take part in their gruesome ceremonies. They seem like something from the witch scares of the sixteenth century, yet they exert their powers today. One of the major studies of Haitian *voodoo* is by Alfred Métraux. In writing about the *zobop* he records a rumour which swept the Haitian capital Port-au-Prince at some unspecified date, perhaps in the early 1940s. This rumour whispered of the *motor-zobop*, an unearthly motor car which drove about at night behind strange blue headlights. A certain Divione Joseph, himself a voodoo magician, suffered a run of bad luck, held to presage some greater calamity.[41]

Travelling home at night, after treating a sick man with

herbs and spells, he had gone to a crossroads, part of an essential ritual to finally cast away the spirits he had drawn from the man's body. Suddenly he was blinded by a blue light. Like the UFO abductees, he lost consciousness, until he came to his senses inside a car. He found himself surrounded by hideous masked beings, who offered him money if he kept his mouth shut, and not tell of what happened to him. The car stopped, he was thrown out. When he recovered again he was in his own bed. Divione's friends insisted that since this experience his character had changed; he became nervous, liable to sudden outbursts of anger or laughter.

This story has many close and obvious parallels with the UFO abductions we have looked at. Firstly, the blinding light and the loss of consciousness are amongst the most frequently reported features of the initial stages of UFO abductions. Subsequent awakening surrounded by strange semi-human figures is common to almost all abduction accounts. Here Divione sees masked men – a sight which would obviously be more familiar to a voodoo practitioner than space-suited aliens. Some other aspects of this Haitian story demonstrate a close relationship to the UFO abductions, particularly in the way the percipient and the abductors behave. There is the basic irrationality of abducting someone, then just offering him money not to tell everyone else about it – the kidnapping appeared to have had no other purpose. This seems rather reminiscent of the activities of the so-called Men In Black – strange people who are alleged to have visited UFO witnesses and researchers, threatening them, or offering them bribes, to remain silent about what they had witnessed or discovered.

Even Divione's intimation that some portentious event was about to happen to him has been put into a ufological context by recent work by the French researcher Jean-Francoise Boedec. In a study of UFO cases in the Finisterre region of Britanny he has introduced the idea of a *'phase d'approche'* or a 'build-up phase'. He claims that

UFO events begin long before the actual UFO puts in its appearance. Days or weeks before then, the witness-to-be starts behaving oddly, breaking usual patterns of behaviour; unusual things start to happen to him. On the night of the sighting he will suddenly feel an urge for a late-night walk, or take a different route home. This seems to have been something that the voodoo practitioners of Haiti, amongst others, have known about for a long time![5]

Abduction rumours

The fear of abduction is a universal and quite natural human fear. It appears in all cultures and strikes at all kinds of people. Usually it is on a personal level – fear for a particular person who is thought to be in particular danger. Sometimes it is more generalized, and often less justified. It can become a rumour sweeping a country, sometimes with fearful consequences. In the nineteenth century, in the cities of Europe, the abduction rumour was based on the fear of 'white slaving'. Innocent women, it was believed, were being snatched from the streets of the cities, in broad daylight, and being led away to a life of prostitution and degradation. The exploits of the white slavers were staple fare for the sensationalist 'police' papers of the time – the *Illustrated Police News* in England, the *Petit Journal* in France, and many others.

While there may well have been cases of such abductions at the time, the sordid reality of the nineteenth-century criminal and sexual underworld was less sensational, if no less appalling, than the popular imagination. The pioneering investigative journalism of the British newspaper proprietor W. T. Stead shows more clearly the real manner of the white slave traffic.

Nevertheless, the rumours took a firm hold on the popular imagination. In the twentieth century the stories grew even more romanticized and remote from reality. Now the innocent victims were being carried off by Valentino-like sheiks. The abduction became the stuff of

The so-called White Slave Traffic was a persistent source of abduction rumour in the early twentieth century. *Above:* illustration from *Le Petit Journal* of the abduction of Cordelia Le Play (1902). *Below:* cover illustration *c.*1930.

romantic fiction, reduced to a mere *frisson*. One writer, under the name of 'Joan Conquest', made a career for herself (or possibly himself) writing gushing tales of abductions by handsome sons of the desert. The tradition lives on in the so-called 'bodice-ripper' school of heavy-breathing historical romance.

But even though diluted and formalized by fifty-odd years of books and films, this rumour can still sometimes flare up and take on a sinister urgency. In 1969 a rumour of abduction swept the city of Orléans but coupled with it was another terrible historical myth that slumbered fitfully beneath the public consciousness – the myth of the Jewish conspiracy.[43]

In the May of that year, girls at schools in the city began to hear, and pass on, stories that a number of fashionable boutiques in the city centre were involved in the kidnapping of young women. The rumours that they heard told of girls who had been trying on dresses in the shops' changing rooms and suddenly vanishing mysteriously. They had been drugged, it was said, bundled out of the shops then smuggled off to Marseilles, destined for North Africa, the Middle East, or elsewhere. The French sociologist Edgar Morin was able to investigate the rumour as it was developing. He suggests in his book *Rumour in Orléans* that the story may have originated via a number of vague press reports about missing women, and an article in a sensationalist tabloid about an abduction that had supposedly taken place in Grenoble at some unspecified date. However it may have started, the rumour evidently touched some deep resonance in the young people who now passed it on. All the shops involved had Jewish proprietors, which lent a disturbing dimension to the story. By 31 May the city of Orléans was in virtual uproar. Crowds clustered outside the shops concerned. The rumours reached peaks of absurdity – all the shops concerned were linked by a network of tunnels that led to the Loire, where a submarine waited to carry off the victims! Sceptics' jokes backfired, to become enmeshed in the story as further evidence of the dastardliness of the plot. The president of a local Jewish association said he mentioned the submarine story as a joke to ridicule the rumour, but the next day had it reported back to him as the sober truth!

What was even more remarkable was the fact that in all this time, *not one woman was reported as missing in Orléans*, even in more down-to-earth circumstances. Eventually, even this fact became part of the rumour, as evidence of the Jewish conspiracy - obviously the press, the police and local officials must have been bribed or threatened. At last official agencies became involved in the affair, and denials and exposures began to appear in the local and regional press. The rumour began to die out and fragment. People denied they had ever believed in the 'ridiculous stories'; but even so, a vague 'no smoke without fire' atmosphere persisted, and related mini-rumours flared up from time to time.

Morin's investigations suggested that the rumour had its origin in the 'white slave' and abduction sub-literature - the works of 'Joan Conquest' and the like - and was fanned by such preoccupations as concern over the sexual permissiveness of the period, and the increased freedom of teenagers - both perhaps symbolized by the type of 'swinging sixties' boutiques on which the rumours centred.

The Hollywood connection

But there are other connections between popular literature, sub-literature and the development of the UFO abduction story. One of the first UFO abduction scenarios occurs, not in the pages of a serious UFO investigation report, but in a Hollywood film. *Invaders From Mars* was a typical small-budget 1950s science fiction B-picture. It had a naive storyline of hideous aliens landing near a small American mid-western town, where they began to control the town's inhabitants by implanting 'control devices' in their necks. This implantation takes place in an operating

Even in the earliest days of science fiction, writers and artists depicted many of the features which were to recur in later UFO and abduction events. Illustration from *L'Invasion Noire* (1895).

theatre inside the alien's spaceship. The whole scene is remarkably reminiscent of the medical examinations reported by the abductees – the alien's captors are held immobile on a table whilst a machine with eye-like devices moves slowly over their bodies.

Other films of the early 1950s show scenes and machines that seem to predate descriptions of similar devices from the abductees of the 1960s and 1970s. Many of the pulp magazines of the pre- and immediately post-war years also seem to have introduced prototypes of many of the features that reappear years later, perhaps on the other side of the world, in 'genuine' close encounter and abduction cases. The 'flying saucer', as a domed, disc-shaped object, itself appeared in SF-pulp literature in the 1930s, years before such devices were ever reported by independent witnesses.

It would be impossible to determine whether or not the abductees and close encounter witnesses had ever seen these films or read these magazines. It would be most unlikely if more than a tiny proportion ever had – the magazines, particularly, were often very obscure and transient. But they all seem to provide evidence of the power of the *idea* of alien abduction – either as an image of terror, or as a harbinger of hope. Just as the science fiction films showed hideous, hostile aliens, they also depicted wise, helpful leaders – *The Day the Earth Stood Still* is a classic of this type; so the fairy kidnappers can be cruel tormentors or bearers of precious gifts; so the aliens from the UFOs can be cold-blooded experimenters, or friends, brothers, who have come to warn and guide us into the future.

Throughout our history, mankind has been beset by mysterious entities who bundle us off to their own secret lairs. But their motives, their methods and their ultimate aims always seem to be hidden and equivocal.

THREE: THE PEOPLE

It has been said that UFOs are implausible things reported by plausible people. But who are the people who say they have been captured by alien creatures? Is there anything that singles these people out as targets for abductions? And what happens to witnesses after they have emerged from their experience? Does this traumatic event have any long term effect on their subsequent lives?

These questions will take us to the heart of the mystery, for they are related to the basic dilemma: is the abduction experience something that happens *to* people; or is it something that people are creating for themselves? If the abductions are being caused by the intervention of some other-worldly force, an examination of the types of people who are being abducted, presumably for scientific investigation, might reveal some clues to the nature and mode of operation of our visitors. Some researchers, both UFO proponents and critics, have rejected the validity of in-depth investigation of the individual witness. The UFO proponents say that if the source of the phenomenon is external, then a study of the witnesses is irrelevant: we should be concentrating our efforts on the phenomenon itself. They argue that the study of the individual fishes that an angler catches will tell us nothing of the personality of the fisherman; the abductees are simply the catch. The UFO opponents take the view that the study of the witness is only needed to filter out the 'unreliable' crank characters, who may be 'polluting' the pool of UFO data with false or dubious claims.

Both these attitudes are wrong. If the UFO abductions are the work of some external or alien force, it is important to know *why* some people are selected for abduction and not others, since this may reveal something of the ultimate aims of the abductors. If the phenomena is actually a result of human delusion or imagination, then the characteristics of the people involved is central to the mystery.

When we make a study of the individuals involved in contact claims we find a few constant characteristics; but we find more things which do not seem to fit into any logical pattern. If the abductees are random specimens for a scientific survey, then the abductors' selection is wide ranging, but would be open to criticism from the big polling organizations.

Our visitors seem to have an overwhelming interest, for instance, in car drivers. The great majority of outdoor abductions are of car drivers, and usually occur at night. Now there does seem to be some logic in this if the abduction phenomenon is a physical kidnapping by aliens. Car drivers are the people most likely to be out in the remoter parts of the countryside late at night, and are thus prime targets if the aliens wish to contact their investigations discreetly without too many witnesses. Yet there are very few cases of remote country dwellers being abducted from isolated farms or homesteads, who might seem to be equally inviting targets.

Although this might seem to present us with an insight into the operational methods of the abductees – their desire for secrecy – it does leave open another explanation. There is a recognized psychological condition known as 'highway hypnosis'. It is caused by the absence of 'sensory input' when driving on long straight roads at night. Very little is happening, the eyes, and other senses are not constantly engaged by changing images and sounds. In these conditions the mind can almost 'switch off', and motorists often suddenly realize that they have passed through towns or villages without remembering anything about it. The Australian researcher Keith Basterfield recalls just such an experience, and records it in his book *Close Encounters of an Australian Kind*:

> One of the worst mental 'jerks' I've ever had was of 'waking' up driving a car at eighty kph along a highway to remember the last twenty minutes of driving. It was along a road I drive every day, and yet couldn't recall that stretch of time. I had quite a fright again when my passenger suddenly said to me, 'Do you remember driving past Reynella?' We had both 'switched off' from noticing the road and the heavy traffic – and we had done so for and at the same period of time. Talking to other drivers I found that this type of experience was not uncommon, especially over short periods of time. Apparently it is even more prevalent for semi-trailer [Dormobile] drivers on long night runs.[4]

So the evidence seems to be pointing in two directions: although night-time abductions of lonely car drivers would seem to be a perfectly logical way for alien abductors to conduct their specimen gathering, it is also open to interpretations in psychological terms, which leave the phenomenon quite Earthbound.

Another important bias begins to show when we examine those abduction cases that have more than one witness. Here we find that in the overwhelming majority of cases the people involved are married, or at the least have strong emotional ties. Now this also seems to have a logical explanation in terms of supposed alien methods of capture. It is likely that people travelling together in cars at night will include a fairly high proportion of married couples, engaged couples, lovers, etc., although the fieldwork which might have to be undertaken to see whether this proportion was as high as that in UFO abductions might be interesting and eventful, to say the least! But again, another explanation can be used to account for this apparent bias.

After an alarming or puzzling event has occurred, people will naturally want to discuss it, and will want to reassure themselves. In the case of people with close emotional links this tendency to reassure each other will be strongest, and each will reinforce the other's perceptions of the events. Often, far from providing reassurance, this sharing of experience will feed on itself to produce an exaggerated and fantasized perception of what was perhaps a quite mundane event. Again, this tendency will be most marked amongst people with close personal relationships, who will probably be less inhibited about expressing fear or alarm to their partners. The overall tendency amongst such reports will be towards a shared experience. Unconsciously, details of an incident perceived or recorded by one of the partners will be accepted by the other as part of their own memory of the experience; eventually the two recollections will coincide, with neither of the pair being able to recall accurately which particular details originate from whose individual experience.

So once again, we are faced with circumstances that fit quite easily into two mutually contradictory frames of reference – the external physical intervention by some unknown agency, or the internal, psychologically reinforced fantasy.

These are, however, a number of well-known abduction cases with two witnesses, where the people involved do not appear to have close, emotional ties.

The so-called 'Pascagoula Case' involves neither drivers, nor a married couple, but just two fishing companions on the banks of the Pascagoula River in Mississippi, in 1973. Charles Hickson and Calvin Parker were spending an October evening fishing off the disused pier of an iron works. They turned when they heard a buzzing noise, and the pair of them were alarmed to see a large, egg-shaped object hovering near them. A door opened in the side of the object, and three figures came out and floated in mid-air towards them. Although basically human-like in outline, they had peculiar featureless faces with conical appendages where their nose and ears should have been. Their arms and legs ended in rounded, crab-like claws. Two of these humanoids grabbed Hickson, the other lifted Parker's arms to carry him, as he had fainted. Hickson was 'floated' rather than just carried into the egg-shaped object. Under later hypnosis, Hickson reported many of the features we have come to recognize as characteristic of the UFO abduction. An eye-like instrument 'scanned' him as he floated in mid-air. The creatures moved him around in front of this object, then left him paralysed, and floating. After a short pause he was 'floated' outside the craft and collapsed to the floor. Here he discovered Parker, on his knees, hysterical and praying. The object then flew away straight upwards. Afraid of ridicule, the two men decided not to report their experience, but later they made a statement to a local airforce base. When their story became public knowledge they were investigated by ufologists from a number of organizations, including the prestigious Center for UFO Studies, who were convinced of the men's sincerity after they underwent lie-detector examination and hypnotic regression.[27]

Although the case is generally touted in the UFO literature as a double abduction, in fact only Hickson was ever hypnotized and gave an account of the inside of the craft. The psychologist conducting the sessions said Parker was still too emotionally disturbed to be put through the hypnotic procedure. However, the initial close sighting was reported by both men.

Sceptical investigators came up with other conclusions, and like so many UFO cases the facts have become inextricably entwined in a tangle of claim and counterclaim, often involving personal and organizational rivalries. Noted UFO debunker James Oberg gives a very different version of the events. He points out that shortly before the reported events, Hickson had been fired for extortion, and immediately afterwards had hired a press agent – it was this agent who had arranged the lie-detector test. He points out that Hickson refused to take an independent test organized later, and tried to interest people in a book or film deal.[44] Hickson's supporters have countered with attacks on Oberg's motives and methods. Hickson has recently confused the issue further by issuing statements claiming further contact with the aliens, and alleging that he is one of the twelve Earth people chosen as liaison between this planet and the aliens. He planned a lecture tour, and a book, saying that the final chapter 'hasn't been written. We're headed for total destruction. The only thing which can help us is something from another world.'[2]

By now one of the cases which could have been a major exception to the general pattern of double-abductions has been so clouded by the dirt stirred up by proponents and sceptics that it is as muddied as the Pascagoula River itself, and virtually useless as evidence either way.

A change of character

Victims of abductions appear to undergo some sort of change after their adventure. Not all become UFO preachers like Charles Hickson; in many cases the changes are quieter, more personal, more concerned with the character and personality of the percipient. This was the case with John and Elaine Avis, the husband and wife involved in the Aveley abduction described briefly in Chapter One.

Following their abduction, both began to exhibit changes in attitude and lifestyle. They both became vegetarians - not through any conscious decision; they simply discovered that they no longer enjoyed eating meat. John became interested in art, a subject he had previously given little thought to. They told investigators that their experience had made them more thoughtful about life and the world. They began to show concern about the ecology movement, nuclear weapons and other political and philosophical issues. It is possible that they would have begun to move in this direction anyway; their experience occurred at a time when there was a general groundswell of interest in these topics in society in general.

But other, more individual, changes in their life also appear to have been a result of the abduction. John, who used to be a heavy smoker, gave up the habit completely, and now cannot even bear the smell of cigarettes. Before the events John had been through a succession of over thirty casual jobs in the building and woodworking trades, in a period of about fifteen years. He has always expressed a dislike of what he calls 'nine to five jobs'.

Born in London's East End, and educated at a state secondary school, he has had the feeling that he has been 'held back' by an inadequate education as a result of large classes and poor teachers. As well as his woodworking jobs he has also worked as a disc-jockey at dances and discos, and for a time was a member of the Small Faces pop group.

By contrast his wife was a more introverted personality. She was educated at a suburban high school in one of the more salubrious Essex commuter areas, leaving to become an accountant. She gave up this job on marriage, and has since been a full-time housewife.

Since the abduction there have been noticeable changes in the couple's characters. John's inability to settle to a regular routine seems to have been channelled into bringing out a suppressed artistic facility. He has taken an art course at a polytechnic, and hopes to go into teaching. He has taken up sculpture, apparently with a certain amount of critical success – at least one of his works has been bought for display in a public building. Elaine also has changed. Beside becoming more self-confident and extrovert, she began attending college and continuing the studies which were interrupted by her marriage.

Their shared interests now appear to be a major part of their life, perhaps providing something to hold in common that was not present in their rather different family and social backgrounds. Consideration of this must prompt the question of the fundamental nature of their shared abduction experience. Were all these changes triggered off by the experience, or is the event itself a result of some emotional crisis or turning point that the couple – consciously or unconsciously – were going through? There is a strong suggestion that the abduction, in this case at least, was a *symptom* of a more personal emotional experience.

The surviving partner of the Hill abduction has also undergone a change in her lifestyle and attitudes since her experience. Betty Hill is now a major figure in the American UFO 'fringe'. From her New England home she now claims to see hundreds of UFOs, and has become the centre of a group which participates in 'skywatches' to spot saucers. Other observers who have attended Betty's skywatches allege that the 'UFOs' she sees are merely distant aircraft, satellites and other easily identifiable phenomena. This, however, does not convince Betty, who now seems to devote a good deal of her life to promoting the UFO cause. Betty Hill appears to have come from a family background of interest in a variety of occult subjects, and commentators have argued that this has influenced her reaction to the UFO incident. Most abductees do not gather small cults around themselves; many are disturbed by the notoriety they attract, and endeavour to sink into a comfortable anonymity. Even John Avis, although he has spoken at UFO gatherings, does not appear to have exploited his experience, nor become the focus of a contactee cult.

There is another factor in the Hill case which some researchers believe is relevant. Betty and Barney were a mixed race couple – she is white, Barney was black – unusual in the atmosphere of New England in the 1950s and 1960s. This must have put considerable emotional strains on both partners, and perhaps set them apart from the society in which they were living. Barney was also active in the black civil rights movement of the period, and this could only have added to their separation from the majority community and put additional strains on them. One writer has gone so far as to suggest that their abduction experience was the traumatized memory of an attack by masked, Ku Klux Klan-type racialists; but there is scant evidence for this, and the close resemblance between the Hills' ordeal and descriptions of other abductions leads most ufologists to conclude that they are all part of the same phenomenon – whatever that may be.

Down in the forest . . .

Although the major preoccupation of many abductees seems to be an attempt to get life back to normal as soon as possible, others have become enmeshed in the resulting series of claims and counter-claims. They feel that it is imperative to prove the validity of their report.

One of the widest publicized abduction reports, perhaps second best known after the Hills, was Travis Walton. Several books have been written about it, including the percipient's own first-hand account, and it received wide publicity in the international press when it happened in 1975.[3]

Walton was a member of a seven-man woodcutting gang, which had a government contract to clear away brushwood in the Apache-Sitgreaves National Park in Arizona. They were driving back to their base after the day's work when they saw a large, luminous object over some trees. They all described it as glowing with a golden light. It was apparently a solid, constructed object with windows, about fifteen to twenty feet across, and shaped like two giant 'pie-pans' placed together, with a smaller bowl shape on top.

Suddenly Walton jumped from the wagon and ran closer to the strange object. The remaining crew members were shouting and pleading with him to come back, when a blue ray suddenly flashed out from the object, and Walton fell to the floor. Driven by fear, his six workmates fled, the badly-sprung van jolting and careering down the bumpy forest track, until they reached the town and returned with the police. But Travis could not be found. Despite extensive searches there was no sign of him for five days until he turned up ragged and unshaven, in a telephone box outside the nearby town of Snowflake.

At once a complex series of events began to unfold. Travis and his brother Duane drove to Phoenix, Arizona, where he was given a polygraph ('lie-detector') test. But far from establishing the truth of Travis's story, the test itself became a subject of controversy. After a visit to a hypnotherapist, retained as a consultant by one UFO research group, Travis denounced him as incompetent. The hypnotherapist suggested that Travis was an habitual drug abuser, and the UFO group that had retained him announced that the abduction was a probable fake. Another group now 'adopted' Travis, and he became another piece of ammunition in the various complicated inter-group rivalries that seem to bedevil serious UFO research in America. Another polygraph test, more favourable to Travis's claims, was immediately denounced by the first group.

UFO sceptics, plaguing both houses, pointed out that the wood clearance gang that Walton had worked with was behind schedule on its contract with the US Forest Service. They hinted that the gang may have thought that a frightening experience like an abduction would furnish a good excuse for welshing on a contract, without financial penalty.[44]

The abductee himself has spent a good deal of time trying to clear his name, and took the fight back to his detractors. Most independent commentators who have met Walton have been impressed with his apparent sincerity, but this is of course a subjective opinion. The chances of ever arriving at the truth behind the Travis Walton Case, as each year passes, and claim and counter-claim are brought out, become increasingly remote.

Walton also seems to have been something of an outsider, living on the margins of society. He had been involved in a couple of small-time robberies when younger, a fact seized on by critics; but he seemed to outgrow this phase, and at the time of his experience was not in any sort of trouble. Critics also pointed out that he and Duane had on several occasions discussed UFOs, and what they might do if they ever confronted one – Travis was strongly for attempting to contact it. The family were regarded as rather 'odd', and his mother had a reputation locally as a psychic and a 'wise-woman' figure – she claimed Indian ancestry. All this must have served to isolate them even more from the strongly Mormon-dominated, closely-knit society of Snowflake.

Canyon contacts

One of the most remarkable, and carefully studied, series of abductions and related experiences in which the characters of the principal participants seem to have been a factor in the nature of the events took place over a period of twenty years in the Tujunga Canyon area of Southern California, in the mountainous hinterland of Los Angeles. At least one of the investigators who interviewed the witnesses has come to the conclusion that the characters of the people involved has a direct and intimate connection with the manner in which their UFO experiences developed.[18]

Sara Shaw and Jan Whitely (the names adopted by the investigators for the two women mainly involved) were aged 21 and 22 and living in an isolated cabin in the Tajunga Canyon. Although just a short drive from the Los Angeles conurbation, the canyon itself is a deserted area, with just a few houses and cabins scattered through a thickly wooded area. The initial events took place in 1953, making this one of the first of the 'modern' abductions we have on record, although the story did not come out until many years later.

The two women lay sleeping in the bedroom of the cabin, when an unnatural stillness and a bright, moving light woke Sara. As she looked through the window the strange glow moved slowly backwards and forwards outside and a beam of light swept the bedroom wall. Terrified, she knelt on the bed, peering out of the window to see the source of the illumination, but it appeared to lie too far beyond the window frame. At first she feared the light might be the headlights of a motor-cycle gang they had seen earlier in the evening come to prey on the isolated pair.

But after a few moments she realized this could not be the case; besides being the wrong colour for headlights, the light was moving to and fro in a smooth, even path, unlike motor-cycles negotiating the rough track. As Jan went to get her dressing gown, Sara glanced at the clock and saw that it was 2 a.m. She felt suddenly giddy and confused; then, looking at the clock again, noticed that the minute hand had moved on twenty minutes. Now both of them were confused, realizing that they must have stood unconscious for twenty minutes. They re-checked the clock and received an even greater shock. Sara was right, the minute hand had moved on to twenty past - but the hour hand had moved on two hours! Two hours and twenty minutes were missing from their lives.

Consumed with panic they fled the cabin, seeking refuge at Jan's foster parents, who lived a few miles away - but not before Jan had seen a curious shadowy figure standing near some bushes outside the cabin.

It was not until many years later, in 1975, that Sara Shaw reported this incident to Ann Druffel, an experienced UFO researcher and writer living in the Los Angeles area. Fascinated by the narrative, and the provocative 'missing time' episode, Ann Druffel arranged a hypnotic regression session, organized by a police psychologist, Dr Reiser. Under hypnosis the now familiar story came pouring out. The 'lights' resolved into a craft. Shadowy, slender creatures carried Sara inside. As she went with them, she saw that Jan was also being taken aboard, but was struggling furiously. Sara allowed herself to be taken quite peacefully.

Inside, Sara was placed on a table and given the almost traditional 'medical examination'. The humanoid figures showed great interest in an operation scar. Further regressions by another hypnotist, Bill McCall, produced more details of her experience.

Jan Whitely's experiences under hypnosis were not so satisfactory from the investigators' point of view. She was unable to give any corroboration of the 1953 event, other than what she could consciously remember before and after the time lapse. But she did begin to reveal hints of experiences which had happened in the years after Jan's abduction. In fact the investigators (Ann Druffel had now been joined by another researcher with special experience in psychic phenomena, Scott Rogo) began to discover that Jan seemed to be the catalyst for a whole series of UFO events involving her and a number of other friends.

The two investigators eventually produced a book*(The Tujunga Canyon Contacts)* detailing the immensely complicated series of contacts, abductions, and bizarre experiences that surrounded a small community of women, apparently centred on Jan Whitely. This led the investigators to two different conclusions. Ann Druffel concluded that the events the women were describing were the result of direct intervention in their lives by paranormal entities that manifested themselves in the forms perceived by the women. She concluded that the women had been singled out for this intervention for two reasons: their interest in psychic and metaphysical studies, and their lesbianism.

It becomes increasingly obvious as one reads Druffel and Rogo's book that the women involved in these events were homosexual. It is strongly hinted that Jan and Sara were involved in a lesbian relationship during their time in the Tujunga canyon in the 1950s. Later, Sara, after an initial unsuccessful marriage, seemed to settle down happily and was no longer plagued by the paranormal phenomena which pursued Jan and her subsequent partners. This led Scott Rogo to a psychologically based explanation of the original experience. He proposes that the original abduction coincided with a time of sexual crisis for Sara, and that her relationship with Jan was ambivalent. He claims that she was trying to break from a lifestyle which both attracted and disturbed her, and says that the UFO abduction represented a 'rape-fantasy', which gave a symbolic form to her own sexual anxieties. He points out details that support this theory: although she is quite calm and goes with the 'men' (though the figures are vague and sketchy, Sara is insistent they are males) voluntarily. Jan, whom she is preparing to leave, struggles against this 'violation'. At one point Sara confessed that she found the 'men's' attentions 'quite fun'. Jan, on the other hand, becomes even more desperate in her struggles when one of the figures touches her breasts. After leaving Jan, Sara's first marriage is to a quadraplegic – Rogo sees this as a further denial of her new sexuality – but then marries again, entering, apparently successfully, a 'conventional' life style.

This psychological interpretation is open to question – some may think it overtly 'sexist' – but there seems to be little doubt that the events described in the abduction story are in some way linked to the sexual dynamics of the women's emotional relationships.

Phoenix in Massachussetts

Another abduction event in which the personality and circumstances of the percipient appears to have been paramount in determining the nature of the experience has become known to ufologists as the 'Andreasson Affair', after the principle protagonist, Betty Andreasson.

On the evening of 25 January 1967, Betty Andreasson was at her home in the town of Ashburnham, Massachussetts, with her parents and her seven children. Her husband James had been injured in a car accident a month before and was still in hospital. At about 6.30 in the evening, there was a pulsating light outside the kitchen window. Betty's father saw some strange looking creatures outside the window, when suddenly Betty saw a number of alien-looking humanoids enter the house through the wall. And that was all Betty remembered for many years.

In 1974 she wrote of her experience to the *National Enquirer*, a tabloid paper which often gave coverage to UFO stories. After they seemed to show no interest, she wrote to Allen Hynek's Center for UFO Studies, who passed it on to another research group, MUFON (Mutual UFO Network). Eventually her story reached Raymond Fowler, a Massachussetts-based UFO investigator attached to MUFON. Finally, in the spring and summer of 1977, more than ten years after the original incident, Betty Andreasson underwent a series of hypnotic regressions to discover what may have happened that January evening.

In regression she reported that four aliens floated through the kitchen door, and lined up before her. They wore dark-blue uniforms with a bird emblazoned on the left sleeve, and a Sam Browne-type belt. Betty at first offered them food, but their leader, who identified himself as Quazgaa, said they needed food for the mind. Betty now handed him a Bible. Quazgaa gave her back a thin blue book.

Now they left the house, and entered an oval craft, which was hovering a few inches above the ground in her back garden. She is taken aboard the craft, is immediately engulfed in a brilliant white light, then told to undress and change into a white garment. She is taken to an examination room, where during the course of her examination a probe is pushed up her nose – 'I heard something break like a membrane or a veil or something, like a piece of tissue they broke through'. Like Betty Hill, another probe is plunged through her navel, and she is told that she is being 'measured for procreation'.

A long and complicated series of events now starts to unfold. Two humanoids take her along a long black tunnel into a compartment containing eight glass-like chairs. She sits on one, and is covered in a fluid. Tubes attached to her mouth and nose enable her to breathe. A sweet, syrupy liquid oozes into her mouth. The liquid drains from the compartment, and the two figures, now hooded, take her through another tunnel. At the end she passes through a glass wall, into an area where everything is red. Strange, small reptile-like creatures are crawling everywhere. Now they pass through another 'membrane' to an area where everything is green. This she finds very beautiful. They float over a pyramid, and see a city of geometric, crystal-like forms.

Betty is taken into one of the crystal structures, where she faces an enormous bird. There is a burst of light and heat, and Betty cries in pain. When the temperature falls the bird is gone. In its place is a mound of embers, from which emerges a 'big fat worm'. Now a voice speaks, and Betty knows that it is the voice of God.

Now Betty and her two 'guides' retrace their steps, back to the glass chair, and the immersion in liquid. Again she tastes the sweet fluid through the tube – she calls out 'Oh, that feels good . . . Oh, this is so good!' She is taken back to the craft, where Quazgaa tells her that 'secrets have been locked in her mind'. Two other aliens take her back to her home, where the rest of her family seem to have been in a state of suspended animation. She has been away three hours and forty minutes. In further hypnotic sessions she gave more details of the various experiences.[21]

These are the bare bones of the narrative; there is much more. Indeed, Raymond Fowler has written two substantial books, *The Andreasson Affair* and *The Andreasson Affair: Phase Two*, describing them in depth. But even from this, we can see that there is a great deal in Betty's account which seems deeply symbolic. There is much overt sexual symbolism, for example. The image of Betty enclosed in a plastic 'bag' immersed in water, and taking nourishment through a tube, is an obvious parallel with the foetus in the womb. There is the constant imagery of penetration – the nose, the navel, the mouth. Even the dressing in white 'examination' robes seems symbolic of a return to purity, which is immediately followed by the nasal 'penetration' and the breaking of a membrane – symbolizing, perhaps, the loss of virginity.

And there is symbolism of a more esoteric nature.

When Quazgaa took the Bible that Betty offered, he produced duplicates of it, thicker than the original, suggesting perhaps some new revelation that is not to be found in the Bible we know. The bird that Betty sees is the Phoenix, burning and being reborn from the ashes.

All the experiences Betty reported, some of which are familiar from other cases, others unique to her, seem in some way connected with the human rather than the extraterrestrial condition. We know that Betty was separated from her husband; we know that later she was divorced and remarried. It is possible that at the time of her abduction Betty was undergoing some sort of personal crisis. We also know that she was a fundamentalist Christian and may have been suffering from a crisis of conscience between her religious beliefs and her sexual or emotional preoccupations. Unfortunately, the investigators of the Andreasson affair have not given us the personal information that allows the psychological insights afforded by the investigators of the Tujunga cases. But we can be sure that the events experienced by Betty Andreasson were in some way personal to her; that they were a working out of a series of half-understood feelings, the prelude, perhaps, to an emotional crisis. What we cannot be sure of is how typical Betty's case is of the abduction phenomenon as a whole. On the surface it seems fairly typical. The changing of clothes and the examination room are repeated time and time again. The bright light is virtually universal. Even the 'immersion' and the umbilical 'feeding tubes' are repeated in other cases, as is being shown a series of strange landscapes. Only the 'phoenix' episode seems unique to Betty's case – even the 'Voice of God' is present in other cases.

And one other point – Betty's marital problems – seems to point to a curious pattern when the individual circumstances of UFO abductees are examined. If we look at those cases where women have been abducted alone, or in the company of other women (ignoring husband and wife cases like Aveley or the Hills), we find a distinct tendency towards the phenomenon selecting women who are divorced, separated or undergoing some sort of marital or sexual crisis.

Besides *The Andreasson Affair*, three popular American books on abductions (*Missing Time* by Budd Hopkins: *Abducted!* by Coral and Jim Lorenzen; and *Direct Encounters* by Judith and Alan Gansberg) give details of eleven women who have described abduction experiences. This table shows their marital condition at the time of the incidents:[24, 31, 38]

Name	*Reference*	*Personal details*
'Patty Price'	Lorenzen	Divorced, with seven children; had just moved to a new house when the experiences began.
Betty Andreasson	Fowler	Married, but husband confined to hospital. Seven children, later divorced and remarried.
Sara Lawson	Lorenzen	Divorced. Casual jobs as singer and waitress. About to take professional examination.
Mona Stafford	Lorenzen	Divorced, unemployed.
Louise Smith	Lorenzen	Widowed.
Elaine Thomas	Lorenzen	Married: no further details.
Lydia Stalnaker	Gansberg	Divorced, two daughters.
'Jessica Rolfe'	Gansberg	Single.
'Virginia Horton'	Hopkins	Married.
'Sara Shaw'	Tujunga	Single. Living in a lesbian relationship, but subsequently married, divorced and remarried.
'Jan Whitely'	Tujunga	Single, lesbian relationship with 'Sara Shaw' at time of first abduction. Other, subsequent experiences.

Thus of the eleven women described in these cases, it

can be seen that four are divorcees, one a widow, and two living in a lesbian relationship. Only two out of the eleven appear to have been married and living with their husbands at the time of the incidents. The sample on which this survey is based is far too small for any conclusions to be drawn: but it does suggest a line of approach for future investigators. In the past, many UFO researchers have neglected to collect personal details of the background of witnesses, feeling that this was not relevant to the subject they were studying. This may be understandable, but it assumes that the UFO phenomenon is external to the witness and quite unconnected with their own personal circumstances. This is far from being proven and there is strong evidence to suggest that the UFO mystery is very much tied up with the individuals who experience it.

FOUR: HARD EVIDENCE

When Harry Joe Turner was kidnapped by the aliens from beyond Alpha Centauri he was driving $80,000 worth of tomato ketchup through Virginia. It was 28 August 1979, about 11.15 p.m., when the lights and engine of his 88-foot rig failed. Neither the AM nor the CB radio would work. Bright lights shone in his rear-view mirror; something dark shot over his cab. Then, although the truck was still coasting at nearly seventy miles per hour, the door flew open and a figure jumped in and grabbed Harry Joe's shoulder. Turner was a hard-bitten truck-driver in a tough business, so he knew just what to do – he pumped eight .32 calibre bullets from his revolver into the intruder, but without seeming to harm his unwelcome passenger. As the truck plunged on into the night, Harry passed out.

Coming round again, he grabbed at the steering-wheel fearing a crash. He then realized, to his bafflement, that he was stationary in the parking lot of his destination in the town of Fredricksburg. Although he had travelled seventeen miles to his destination he claimed that fuel for a 117 mile trip had been used up. The end of one of the radio aerials looked burned, another was sheared off, a thin film of material covered the cab. When he started to drive back home, he passed out again. This time when he came to, he was in a local hospital.

Gradually, his memory of the missing time returned,

without the need for any hypnotic regression. His first memory, after he had tried to shoot the intruder, was of the whole truck being lifted into a giant craft hovering overhead. Here he met humanoid entities, dressed in white clothes and caps which covered their ears. Like several other abductees, he claimed that he was operated on, and that something was implanted in the left side of his chest which gave the aliens control over the whole of that side of the body. Then he was taken on what seemed a guided tour of the cosmos – he was shown Neil Armstrong's first footprint on the Moon, and taken to futuristic domed cities on a planet light years beyond Alpha Centauri.

After this initial experience, he claimed more contacts with the aliens, and alleged that he had gained psychic powers. He took an interest in religion; never before a churchgoer, he began to attend church regularly, studied the Bible, and searched religious literature for a meaning to his experience.

But what of the physical evidence that might have helped prove his story? The two damaged antennae were studied at a materials testing laboratory. The end of the CB aerial revealed saw marks that could have been produced by a hacksaw, and the burnt ends had been charred with heat applied from a concentrated source, such as a blowlamp.

The people who know Turner have conflicting views of his story. Some of his workmates completely discount it, claiming that he is only spreading the tale because he 'wants to be bigger than he is'. Others who know him accept that he honestly believes what he says happened to him, whatever that may be. But the hard evidence, the pieces that can actually be handled, examined and analyzed, reveals nothing.[29]

Backing up the witness

The evidence presented so far for the reality of UFO abductions has been based on the testimony of individual witnesses and abductees. The weight investigators place on this kind of evidence is dependent on two factors: the reliability of the individuals concerned and our assessment of their character and truthfulness, our estimation of what they have to gain or lose by making the claims they do. Secondly, investigators will look at how well their evidence is corroborated by other witnesses to the events they were involved in, or how well their testimony relates to other information received about other, similar events.

Most assessments of the value of a particular piece of evidence are usually concentrated on the consideration of the reliability of the witness. It has always been held that some types of people may be more honest or reliable witnesses than others. In the consideration of the PC Godfrey abduction in Chapter One, we saw how ufologists were more likely to be impressed by a policeman as a witness, because the constraints and responsibilities of his job would be likely to preclude frivolous reports. Similarly, an airline pilot is a trained observer, who might be expected to be rather more accurate than the lay person when it comes to making accurate estimates of speed, distance or direction. The evidence from such people, and others whose word can be respected, has formed the greater part of the evidence for the UFO phenomenon.

But when we start to look for 'hard evidence' we begin to encounter further problems. It is one of the primary aims of UFO researchers to encourage the broader scientific community to undertake an objective study of the phenomenon. In order to do this the scientists, particularly those in the physical sciences such as physics, chemistry, biology, etc., will ask for something that they can study, something that is still around when the UFO has departed. This 'something' could be a specimen of metal, a manufactured artefact, a chemical residue, or an image on a photographic emulsion. But it must be something that they can take into their laboratories and study. Providing this evidence has proved to be the most difficult part of the ufologists' task.

The single biggest category of 'hard evidence' is the collection of photographs that has built up over forty years, purporting to shown UFOs in flight or on the ground. Probably the vast majority of them are photographs of normal things taken under abnormal conditions, or flaws in film emulsions or introduced during the processing. Some are undoubted frauds. Others may represent unusual natural phenomena, accidental double exposures and other intentional and unintentional photographic aberrations. Of the few which pass most of the checks it is quite likely that a further proportion could be disposed of similarly if there were more information to hand. It is a distressing fact that there are very few, if any, photographs that are universally accepted as 'genuine' even amongst UFO proponents. In many cases the arguments between groups promoting and debunking a particular photograph seem to take on more significance than the phenomenon itself. There are a number of long-standing feuds between UFO groups over well-known photographs.

In view of all this it is hardly surprising to find that no abduction case has yielded any photograph that has stood up to close investigation, and in fact very few abductees have presented any photographic evidence at all. In the early years of the UFO controversy there were a number of photographs purporting to show spacemen and saucers, mostly produced by the 'contactees'. But none of these is now taken seriously by modern researchers.

Although in the more general UFO field there are a small number of photographs that seem to satisfy quite rigorous criteria and apparently portray some kind of unidentified phenomena, in the abduction field the photographic evidence is virtually non-existent.

Similarly, there are very few manufactured articles that have ever been presented as evidence of UFO contacts, although there have been one or two cases of contactees or abductees attempting to remove some small object from the UFO as evidence. Antonio Villas Boas tried to smuggle out a small clock-like instrument (Chapter Two), but was foiled by his captors, who snatched it from him. Physical evidence of this type has been rather more a feature of the non-abduction 'contact' cases. Sometimes a witness to such an event has come away with a piece of metal with curious marks on it, or some small, unidentifiable machine component.

One of the oddest items ever offered as evidence of contact with extraterrestrials was a pancake! In April 1961, Joe Simonton, a chicken farmer living in Wisconsin, looked out of his farmhouse window to see a silvery machine landing in his backyard. A hatch slid open and three men, five feet tall, wearing blue uniforms and 'balaclave helmets' stepped out. One held out a bucket, and indicated that he wanted Joe to fill it with water, which he did from the farmyard pump. As he returned the bucket to the man he saw one of the other figures inside the craft was working at a kind of stove, and had a pile of pancakes next to it. The first man picked four up and gave them to the farmer. The hatch closed and the craft moved off slowly into the air, leaving a bemused chicken farmer holding four warm pancakes. Researchers cautiously nibbled one and reported that it tasted like cardboard. A chemical analysis showed that it was a pancake - a perfectly normal oatmeal pancake. Now this might prove that Joe Simonton was a fraud. On the other hand it might prove that pancakes are pretty much the same wherever they come from. Or it might prove that humanoid creatures from other worlds can exist quite happily on Earth foods when they have to do so through force of circumstances![6]

In a way this is typical of the equivocal nature of the physical evidence from UFO contacts. In most cases it can provide ammunition for proponents and debunkers. And like the photographic evidence, there is probably no single piece of evidence that is accepted universally by the ufologists themselves - let alone convince sceptical scientists.

Marks and traces

Sometimes the 'hard evidence' takes the form of marks or traces, which have allegedly been left behind at the site of UFO landings and encounters. These can take several forms. Most common, probably, are the 'landing marks'. These are usually depressions made in the soil or vegetation corresponding to the legs of UFO 'landing gear'. One American researcher has compiled a catalogue of several hundred instances of these physical traces.

A serious problem with this particular type of evidence is that it is often not found until some time after the initial event is reported, often when researchers are searching the encounter site. It is possible that on many occasions other, unrelated, markings are wrongly attributed to the UFO. In most cases witnesses are either too far away or too confused to record exactly where the UFO has actually landed, so there is an understandable tendency for *any* markings in the vicinity - perhaps caused by farm machinery, building plant or the like - to be interpreted as 'landing marks'. In some cases curious marks or depressions on the ground are identified immediately as landing traces even when *no* UFO has actually been reported. This has happened a lot in UFO flap areas - places where there has been a rush of reports in a small area over a short period of time. In the 1960s British ufologists argued at great length over a small hole that appeared in a potato field in Wiltshire. Numerous claims and counter claims were bandied about, attributing it to everything from a lightning strike to a giant spaceship from Uranus. Yet at no time had a UFO been reported anywhere near the site!

From time to time other 'physical traces' are reported from UFO encounter sites. These include a white powdery material and an unpleasant oily substance. Again, there has been considerable controversy over the identification of these traces. On some occasions they have been analyzed and found to be types of fungus or plant moulds; at others they have been revealed to have been of inorganic origin. But in no case has any definitely exotic origin been proved.

Other physical traces associated with landings or low-level UFO events include damage to trees and vegetation, the heating or 'baking' of plant roots, or damage to buildings. Although all these effects have been reported in connection with UFO events of all kinds, very few have ever been associated with abduction cases, and this has led some ufologists to suggest that the abduction event may be a different type of phenomenon from most of the other UFO cases.

Evidence from animals

One type of effect on the environment which is common to abduction and other UFO reports involves wild and domesticated animals. These cases are particularly significant in the context of the abduction reports. They seem to fall into two categories. The first is where the animals react with alarm or fear, apparently in response to the approach of the UFO. Dogs growl, hackles are raised; domestic fowl rush about madly. Often the human witness is alerted to the presence of the UFO in the first place by the odd reaction of nearby animals.

Veteran British UFO researcher Gordon Creighton, working for the magazine *Flying Saucer Review*, compiled a catalogue of over 200 such cases reported in UFO books and magazines. These are typical:[16]

> In Malta, Montana, USA, in January 1967, a farmer and his wife were alerted by the barking of their dog, and saw a large, rectangular object with red and amber lights moving rapidly in the distance to land finally in a field.

> In the British UFO 'flap' of 1967 an object with windows, purple and green lights, passed over the town of Hindley, Lancashire, making a loud buzzing noise. The object alarmed dogs, which barked loudly and rushed about.

> In November 1967 a Romanian farmer 'suddenly saw all the chickens in my farmyard running towards me, cackling like lunatics . . . visibly terrified . . . I raised my head and clearly saw a very brilliant object, silver or aluminium in the shape of a disc . . .'

In all these cases it is assumed that the odd behaviour of the animals is a direct result of the presence of a strange aerial object. Although it might be expected that any unusual or noisy object might disturb animals, it is often the case that the phenomenon apparently producing these reactions is very distant or silent. Many animals have sensory powers far in excess of anything humans possess – the radar-like hearing of bats, the apparent sensitivity of migrating birds to the Earth's magnetic field. It might seem likely, then, to suppose that even quite small changes in the immediate environment that might be caused by a UFO could be registered by the sensory apparatus of some animals, before becoming discernible to human witnesses. There are a number of other reasons why this testimony from animals should be held as evidence pointing to the physical presence of some unidentified phenomena. Animals do not share the fantasies and assumptions that humans are prone to. Although a human witness might hallucinate a strange event or encounter, it is not likely that a nearby animal will react to the same psychological stimulus, so any animal reaction is strong evidence of the presence of some physically real stimulus, even if the human then goes on to fantasize from that. Against this one must remember that some animals, particularly domestic pets, can be very sensitive to the mood and emotions of humans. A dog acting wildly, barking and jumping about, may just be responding to its master's strange behaviour, rather than detecting something strange itself.

Like so much of the evidence for UFOs and UFO abductions, we are so often left depending on the evidence of the single witness. It is, after all, a part of the witness' testimony that animals in the neighbourhood are acting strangely, and it is nearly always the witness's assumption that this behaviour was triggered off by the UFO phenomenon that the human is reporting. A leading American UFO researcher Allan Hendry, in his important book *The UFO Handbook*, has shown that similar animal reactions have been reported even in cases where the apparent 'UFO' has been definitely identified as some conventional object. He quotes an amusing example from his own experience when, seeing the lights of an approaching plane, he joked to a companion that a UFO was approaching them. At that very moment all the dogs in the vicinity started barking.[30]

The second type of unusual animal behaviour has been reported in many abduction and close encounter cases, and has become something of an indicator of this kind of case. These are cases that recall the Sherlock Holmes story, where the detective remarks on the peculiar behaviour of the watchdog in the night. 'But the dog did nothing,' protests Dr Watson. 'That,' retorts Holmes, 'was the peculiar behaviour!'

A case reported from Maine in 1975 concerns two young men, identified by the investigators only as 'P' and 'W'. The men shared a mobile home near the town of Norway. Both had night jobs, so it was not unusual that they were awake and listening to music at 3 a.m. They heard an explosion, but when they rushed outside they could see nothing. However, as they were then up and about they decided it would be a good idea to take a short drive down to a nearby lake. After they had been driving for a short while they began to be 'buzzed' by a luminous UFO that flew around their car, almost giving an aerobatic display. This was joined by other, smaller, lights, which behaved in the same manner. At one point, after being almost blinded by 'the brightest lights I ['W'] ever saw', they suddenly found themselves a mile away from the last point they could remember.[20]

In the time immediately before and after this 'display',

although they saw or heard no evidence of the nocturnal animal life of the woods, they did notice a herd of cows in a field sitting on the ground, and shaking their heads from side to side.

They did not tell anyone else of the experience, but began to notice a number of symptoms – lightheadedness, burning eyes, sore mouths, a discoloration of the skin around the eyes, and of their tongues. Subsequently, both young men underwent a series of 'paranormal' events, including more sightings of aerial lights, and even more curious manifestations indoors, including the appearance of a cube-shaped object which seemed to disappear through a wall.

'W' agreed to undergo hypnotic regression in an attempt to discover what had happened when their car had apparently travelled a mile without their remembering anything about it. As his story emerged under hypnosis, 'W' found himself in a room looking through a window at his car on the ground below him. 'P' was still inside. There was a door in the room, the walls of which narrowed as they rose. 'W' was joined by a strange, non-human entity, clad in 'what looked like a sheet' (compare this with PC Godfrey's description of the clothes worn by 'Joseph' in his encounter). The being had large slanted eyes, a small nose, and apparently no mouth on a 'mushroom shaped' head. He was taken to another room set out like an operating theatre. Here similar creatures attempted to examine him (they took a blood sample with a needle-like apparatus), but when they tried to make him lie on the table, he hit one of them in the face. Eventually he did lie on the table, where he was stripped and examined with the aid of a square instrument with gauges and controls. The creatures communicated with him, apparently telepathically, then after dressing he was taken back to the first room, then suddenly found himself back in the car.

The lack of animal life and absence of birdsong is a recurrent feature in UFO close encounter cases. It has been suggested that, like alleged animal disturbance at the presence of a UFO, wild creatures are silenced or driven away from the vicinity of a UFO by some form of radiation or other influence – microwaves and ultrasonic vibrations have been suggested. This may be so, but it would not explain another related phenomenon that is often reported in these cases. Not only are birds and animals conspicuously absent, but humans are too!

Although not strictly an abduction case, the experience of a young couple – 'Peter' and 'Frances' – in Rhodesia (Zimbabwe) in 1974 has many features in common with the classic abductions. The 30th of May was the eve of a national holiday, and the couple were driving to Durban, South Africa, via the border town of Beit Bridge. As they drove through the night they became aware of a light apparently pacing their car. As it closed in on them their lights began to fail, and the car felt very cold. Peter took his feet off the pedals, but to his astonishment the car kept going, as if under some sort of remote control. After a series of unearthly adventures (at one point they appeared to be driving through a landscape which they knew did not exist along that route) they arrived at Beit Bridge, 400km from their starting point. Now this was in 1974, a time when Rhodesia was subject to international sanctions. South Africa was the only neighbouring state that kept an open border with Rhodesia, and most of that country's trade went through its southerly neighbour. The road from Salisbury to Beit Bridge was the main route for most of this trade, as well as for holidaymakers. Yet throughout the whole of their strange journey Peter and Frances saw no other vehicle or person, except for an empty bus parked in a lay-by.

Time and again in abduction and close encounter cases we read of witnesses stopping by the side of busy roads for hours at a time, yet seeing no other traffic. This can hardly be as a result of emanations from a UFO forcing motorists away from a particular stretch of road; apart from anything else, we would undoubtedly have other, independent evidence of such a thing happening. Again we are faced with the conclusion that this particular piece of evidence is dependent totally on the testimony of the individual involved.[51]

The case of 'W' and 'P' in the Maine incident presents another piece of 'hard evidence', which exists for some time after the immediate event is over and can be examined by researchers. Both men reported a number of physiological effects – skin discoloration, burning eyes, soreness, etc. In many cases symptoms like these are the first sign that an apparently unexceptional UFO sighting has a more significant character.

In the classic Betty and Barney Hill case, one of the first indications that there was more to the incident than was first suspected was when Barney developed a ring of warts around his genitals, apparently corresponding to the position of the cup-like object which his abductors placed there.

Following his encounter with the seductive young lady on the UFO in Brazil, the farmer Antonio Villas Boas experienced some of the symptoms which have subsequently become typical of close encounter witness reports. Dr Olavo Fontes, a Brazilian physician who examined him when he came forward with his story, recorded that after the events Villas Boas suffered from loss of appetite, a burning sensation in his eyes, excessive tiredness and the discoloration of the skin on parts of his face. These effects are remarkably consistent in many similar cases, and are evidence for the existence of some common origin for these reports. But it is significant that most, if not all, of these symptoms are also those most characteristic of psychosomatic illnesses, where the outward, bodily symptom is created by the patient's mental condition. Blotchy and discoloured skin, rashes, and other skin complaints like eczema, are very often the result of severe emotional conditions in the patient, rather than symptoms of an organic nature. Other typical symptoms, such as soreness of the eyes or discoloration or soreness of the membrane in the mouth, can also be linked with psychosomatic conditions, and warts are notoriously susceptible to mental state – most of the 'old wives cures' will work if the sufferer actually believes they will.

Double abductions

Budd Hopkins is an American artist who became fascinated by the stories of the UFO abductees, initially after a chance meeting with one of the victims. In a series of investigations, carried out through the use of hypnotic regression, he uncovered a remarkable series of 'coincidences' linking several abductees, all of whom displayed a common physiological after-effect from their experiences.[31]

Hopkins, and his hypnotist colleague Dr Aphrodite Clamar, were investigating 'missing time' experiences as reported by a number of different people. But as they talked further to their subjects, almost accidentally a pattern began to emerge. Some people reported that the abduction under study was in fact the *second* time they had had such a strange experience. Each of them remembered that at some time in their childhood they had suffered an odd, and particularly deep, cut in their leg. At the time they had no recollection at all of how such a drastic wound had been caused; they or their parents could find no indications of where the cut might have been accidentally inflicted. There were no bloodstains where the child had been playing, and the wound was noticeably clean and uninfected.

Dr Clamar regressed her subjects back to this childhood experience, and stories emerged of a first abduction at the age of about seven. They revealed that as children they had been taken aboard a strange craft and, as in the later experience, they were laid on an 'operating table'. But on this occasion their alien abductors used an instrument to cut deeply into their leg. All four of the witnesses Hopkins studied still bore the scars of this cut.

Even more remarkably, all of these people were born in 1943 and underwent their strange operation in the summer of 1950, at the age of seven. This series of events seems to provide the best evidence for some kind of hard reality behind the mystery of the abductions. Details of the type of entity, the description of the 'craft' and the form the 'operation' took tally closely in all four accounts. The scars provide physical evidence that *something* objective and real happened; but it is impossible to say just what that something was, unless and until more such cases begin to be uncovered by other, independent investigators.

Charting the evidence

Objective proof of a genuine, apparently extraterrestrial, origin for the UFO and abduction phenomenon need not be in the form of a solid piece of metal or a captured alien. Sceptical researchers have pointed out that *information* can constitute hard evidence. If an abductee were to return from his or her experience with some piece of information, some scientific fact that was not previously known but that could subsequently be confirmed, then this would be powerful evidence that the experience was not confined to the mind of the percipient.

Some of the early contactees did claim to have acquired hitherto unknown information. Unfortunately, this was either totally nonsensical, or impossible to confirm – or both! Adamski, for instance, claimed that the far side of the moon was a lush inhabited land, with fertile vegetation, rivers and cities. Some of his followers managed to believe this, until the first space-probes began to report a world as barren as the half of the Moon which faces us. (Some of the contact cultists still believe in an inhabited Moon, claiming that the pictures from American and Soviet space-craft are fakes, engineered to hide *The Truth*!)

Much of the 'information' presented by contactees and abductees is unprovable and undisprovable – descriptions of the 'home planets' of the aliens for instance. As these are usually described as being thousands of light years away from Earth, we are going to have to wait rather a long time before we can confirm or deny the accuracy of their statements!

However, not all of the information produced is quite so far beyond serious scientific analysis. One piece of evidence in particular has been subjected to very close and careful scrutiny, by both proponents and opponents of the extraterrestrial theory of UFO origin. The information was provided by Betty Hill, from her famous abduction in 1961. Although much of the information about this case derives from the hypnotic sessions she and her husband Barney underwent, more came from conscious recollections which began to surface after the sessions. At one point Betty described a screen-like object on the wall of the room they were being held in. It bore a series of light points joined by lines of varying thickness. Betty became sure that this was a 'star map', recording the interstellar travels of the race of beings who abducted her. Two large lights, which had the thickest lines radiating from them seemed to mark their 'home planet'. Betty described the positions of the stars and lines in great detail, and some investigators began a search to see if this particular configuration did in fact correspond with any actual known configuration of stars. If such an arrangement could be found, and if it could be determined that the stars so revealed were liable to have planets capable of bearing life, this could be powerful evidence for the reality of interplanetary visitors.

A schoolteacher, Marjorie Fish, began the massive task of searching through the nearest stars to the Earth in the hope of finding an arrangement which matched the star map. She began by literally producing a model of the universe within forty-five light years of the Sun, using beads hanging on pieces of thread to represent stars. At first no pattern resembling the map could be discerned. Then she decided that all the non-sunlike stars should be removed, as these were the ones least likely to be supportive of planets with humanoid inhabitants as described by Betty Hill. Eventually a pattern was identified, which centred on the two stars Zeta Reticuli 1 and 2, small stars in the constellation of the Net, which is not

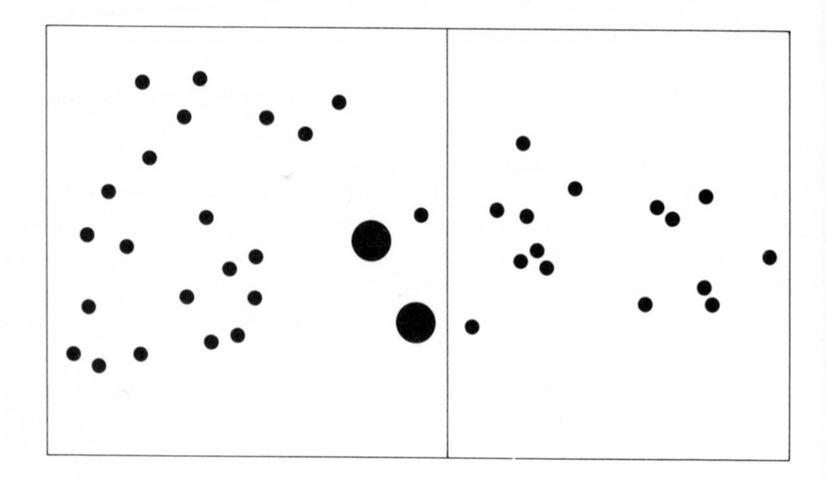

Above: The Hill 'star map' (left) and the Marjorie Fish interpretation (right) without 'trade routes' linking the stars.

Below: The Hill map (left) and the Fish interpretation (right) with linking 'trade routes'.

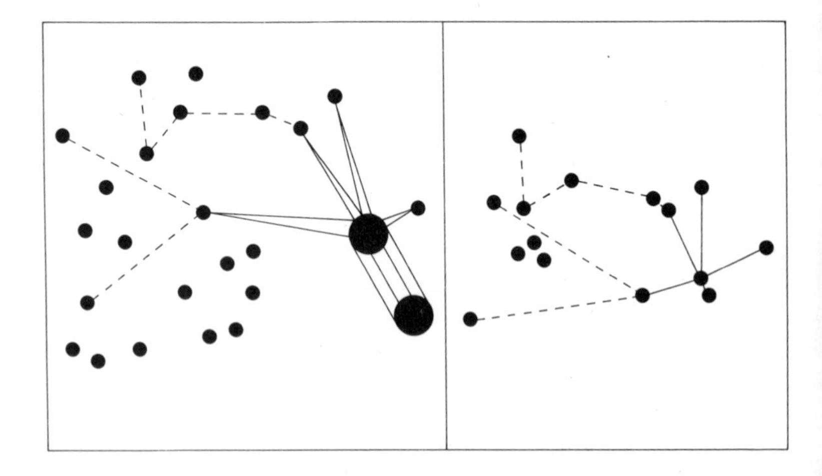

visible from the Northern Hemisphere.

Critics pointed out that given the enormous volume of space which was available to be drawn on for the search (Marjorie Fish's forty-five light year limit was quite arbitrary) it would not be surprising if some sort of correspondence was to be found. Astronomer and UFO sceptic Carl Sagan noted that the correspondence was not that close anyway, and if the helpful 'trade-routes' were removed few people would notice any resemblance between the Fish and the Hill maps. The diagrams opposite show the Hill map (top left) and the Fish map (top right). For comparison the maps are also shown *with* the appropriate lines added (opposite, below left and right).

However, proponents of the validity of the maps pointed out that of more than 100 stars in the volume of space covered by Marjorie Fish, only twelve are sunlike, and *all* these go into making up the pattern connected up by trade routes. Moreover, these routes make logical sense, and join the stars concerned up without backtracking in three dimensions from one side of the space to the other.

In 1980 a group of astronomers published the result of their findings following the use of a new technique which identified double stars which were too close to be distinguished by optical telescopes. This they claimed, revealed that Zeta Reticuli 2, the alleged home planet of the aliens, was actually a double star. This had serious implications. Firstly, why would the Reticulans show their home system as a single star on maps aboard their own ship? But more damningly, Marjorie Fish had herself excluded double stars from her calculations, on the entirely justified grounds that planetary orbits around them would be too unstable to allow the development of life over millions of years.

The argument was rejected by defenders, who criticized the still experimental techniques used by the astronomers who claimed to have discovered the binary nature of Zeta

Reticuli 2. It was pointed out that in the case of very closely linked double stars it might still be possible for stable planetary orbits to develop.

So the debate over the Fish star map seems to have ground to a halt in that no-man's-land between believer and sceptic. Its fate seems to have followed the pattern of so many of the arguments over the physical evidence, which seems to support all sides, with every assertion being challenged and the prospect of a tidy answer receding ever further.[22]

Witnessing the witness

Hard evidence could also be independent testimony - a witness unconnected with the abductee, who sees and reports the abduction event. Perhaps a passer-by who happens to see the victim being led, carried, or pushed into the waiting alien craft. Unfortunately, such convenient passers-by seem to be totally absent from the reports we have. Most multi-witness events are those involving two or more abductees: the Hickson and Parker case in Pascagoula, Betty and Barney Hill, the abductions in Tujunga Canyon. As we have seen, these cases cannot be said to furnish truly *independent* testimony, for usually the witnesses share the experience, including all its strongly subjective aspects.

One of the best witnessed cases was the Travis Walton abduction in Arizona. We have already seen how Walton was with six other men, who saw him being knocked to the ground by a blue beam from a hovering UFO. The men drove off in panic, before returning later with police. They did not actually see what happened after he had fallen to the ground. Was he then bundled up into the object by alien creatures? Did he lie for a while on the forest floor, then wander off aimlessly, his memory blocked by some massive neurological disruption, the emptiness to be filled by a fantasy of aliens? Or did he sit for a while, smiling to himself before hurrying off to a prepared hiding place, while a world-wide furore developed around him?

Even if we reject the allegations thrown by critics that the whole incident was an elaborate ruse cooked up by the workmen to provide an excuse for failure to meet contract deadlines, we are left with six witnesses to a spectacular UFO event, but none at all to a UFO abduction.

The case of policeman Alan Godfrey was also described as having independent corroboration. The investigators pointed out that other police officers also saw a UFO at the time of Godfrey's encounter. But these policemen were at Halifax, nearly ten miles across the Pennines from Godfrey's home town of Todmorden, and they had merely seen strange lights heading off in that direction. Whilst their description might give some extra weight to Alan's otherwise unsupported testimony, it cannot be seen as corroboration.

Of course, this absence of independent eyewitnesses does not actually *prove* anything one way or the other about the abduction phenomenon. Those who support the idea that the abductions are the work of an extra-terrestrial race can simply point out that it is hardly surprising that such a programme of abduction would be conducted at times and places when there were no other witnesses about. It might be in the interests of these aliens to keep humankind totally in the dark about these operations.

The 'electromagnetic effect'

There is one other way in which the close approach of a UFO is reported as having a physical effect on the immediate environment. Many close encounter witnesses have noticed that the presence of the UFO seems to produce an effect on electrical apparatus. We have already seen instances where the witnesses' first intimation of the onset of some odd phenomenon has been when their cars suddenly lose power, or in some instances are apparently 'taken over' by an external force – the cases at Aveley and Beit Bridge, Rhodesia, are typical.

This phenomenon has been long known to ufologists

and is generally known as the 'electromagnetic effect', as this has been assumed to be the mechanism involved.

In the late 1960s the American Government, prompted by public concern over a wave of UFO reports, commissioned the University of Colorado to prepare an analysis of the UFO phenomenon. Generally known as the 'Condon Report' after its chairman, physicist Edward U. Condon, this report was highly critical of research into UFO reports, and was itself attacked by many ufologists as a debunking attempt to cover up the 'real' UFO mystery. However, as part of their investigations they undertook a number of scientific tests on various pieces of hard evidence, one of which was a car that had been involved in a UFO 'car stop' incident.[14]

Each car, when it is made, acquires a particular pattern of magnetism in the metal from which it is made. This is similar in all cars of the same make. The Condon investigators thought that if a vehicle had been subjected to a powerful magnetic force, sufficient to affect the engine or electrical system, this 'magnetic signature' would be radically changed. This had not happened to the car they examined. Although this eliminated one possible mechanism for the car-stop effect, it did not in itself disprove the UFO witnesses' reports. But again, it means that the evidence is reduced to accounts given by the individual involved.

In the years after the Condon Report, a number of ufologists began to investigate some of the UFO/folklore links outlined in Chapter Two. They began to find instances of strange vehicle stoppages from before the internal combustion engine – a cart that could not be moved by horses or a team of men in the vicinity of a house plagued by a poltergeist. Long before UFOs were stopping cars, witches were stopping farmers' carts, and as recently as the First World War it was alleged that it was unlucky to take a wheeled vehicle into the Essex village of Canewdon because they would invariably break down or puncture. In the same area, just a few years earlier, an old villager was credited with the power to stop farm machinery simply by looking at it.[40]

A number of UFO reports and abduction narratives have told of how radio and television have been interfered with in the presence of a UFO. This is something that is particularly hard to quantify. There are many sources of such interference, and although some radio interference cases have been corroborated by a number of independent witnesses, which strongly suggests that some external physical force was present, it is a very long jump from that to proof of a 'solid' UFO. Some ufologists have suggested that many otherwise inexplicable UFOs may be the result of a rare meteorological phenomenon created by forces from the Earth's magnetic field. Although this theory presents many problems of its own, it would provide an explanation for the electrical and magnetic anomalies that appear to crop up in a percentage of UFO and abduction reports.

All the 'hard evidence' that has been presented, on close examination, begins to develop soft edges. None of it seems to provide the final, undeniable proof of a 'real' extraterrestrial UFO. Yet the evidence keeps building up; in case after case, the same features, the same pieces of evidence, are alleged. Like so much else in the abduction mystery, the hard evidence is equivocal; it can be used to support or deny any aspect of the phenomenon.

Despite years of painstaking work by researchers, we are left with the testimony of the witnesses, the implausible things reported by plausible people, on which we have to build our explanations.

FIVE: THE SEARCH FOR EXPLANATIONS

The most widely accepted theory for the origin of the forces behind the UFO abductions did not have to be sought for. It was thrust upon the first researchers by the phenomenon itself. The agents who were abducting human beings identified themselves – they were extraterrestrials. In case after case the abductors announced that they came from another planet. In some cases they even took their involuntary guests there.

The extraterrestrial hypothesis (generally referred to by UFO investigators as the 'ETH', a convention I shall adopt henceforth) was not so obvious when the UFO phenomenon itself began to take shape in the 1940s. The explanation that many people accepted at that time was that these strange craft were some sort of earthly secret weapon – from Russia, the USA or some other totally terrestrial nation. Surprisingly, this idea still has its adherents, many of whom propose such exotic variants as secret weapons from hidden Nazi bases in the jungles or pampas of South America, or the emptiness of the Antarctic.

However, as more came to be known publicly about the potentialities of space travel, as it was being developed in America and Russia, the idea rapidly spread amongst those who interested themselves in the new study of 'ufology' that the reports of UFOs were reports of craft whose performances and construction were well beyond the capabilities of any earthly science. The ETH was almost universally accepted as the most probable explanation for the saucers.

The reports confirmed this. Many of the close encounter cases presented clear and unambiguous descriptions of solidly constructed vehicles. Those witnesses who reported actually seeing the occupants of the crafts noted that many of these creatures were engaged in such activities as collecting earth or plant samples, operating machinery or instruments, or apparently observing and recording environmental data.

In 1965 a French lavender-grower on the Valensole plateau in southern France, Maurice Masse, encountered a group of small creatures, and their landed craft, apparently taking samples of the lavender plants in his fields. These creatures, less than four feet tall, had very large, round heads, and the large elongated eyes, slanting way round the sides of their heads, that we now see as a characteristic of many of the aliens involved in the abduction cases. One of these creatures pointed an instrument at Masse, which appeared to paralyze him. After a while the creatures entered their machine, which then shot off. It certainly looks possible that, in this instance, the visitors were carrying out a survey of the flora of central France – perhaps if the fauna had been on their programme too, we might have had another abduction case![8]

It is noteworthy that these cases were happening in the years when a great deal of effort was being put into mounting an expedition to the Moon, and just a few years later space-suited humans would be moving clumsily round on another world, doing much the same sort of things as some of our visitors were alleged to be doing. The idea of a *quid pro quo*, an alien survey of Earth, was convincing and timely.

One of the factors that points most strongly towards an ETH type of explanation for the abductions is the remarkable consistency of many of the accounts. In this book, we have seen cases that show a remarkable similarity of detail. Many of the abductees report quite small details that correspond with descriptions from other cases by witnesses on the other side of the world. This has helped to support the thesis that there is some common cause behind these cases.

The physical descriptions of the humanoid creatures involved in the abductions show a remarkable consistency throughout many cases. They are described, for the most part in two ways, and they could perhaps be inhabitants of two planets with slightly different environments. One group of beings seems to consist of rather small creatures, less than five feet in height, with large heads, extremely large eyes, and almost insignificant noses and mouths. These beings are usually described as having long fingers, and wearing dull or silvery coloured coveralls. The creatures met by Travis Walton in his controversial 1975 abduction (Chapter Three) are typical of this type:

> They were very short, shorter than five feet, and they had very large bald heads, no hair. Their heads were domed, very large . . . They had . . . enormous eyes, almost all brown, without much white in them . . . The creepiest thing about them were those eyes . . . Their mouth and ears and noses seemed real small, maybe just because their eyes were so huge . . . They had this white, marshmallowy-looking skin, and their bodies were real lightweight . . . They were wearing loose coveralls kind of an orangish-tannish-brown . . . I didn't see any zipper, no buttons . . .

These descriptions are consistent with descriptions given by other abductees, and also by witnesses who have experienced other types of close encounters with UFO-related entities. The detailed description given by farmer Maurice Masse of the creatures he found taking such an interest in his lavender crop serves to corroborate the descriptions of the abductees:

> Their bodies [were] the size of an eight-year-old child, and their

enormous heads [were] three times the size of a normal human head . . . the skin [was] as smooth as a baby's and white – at any rate the skin of the face and the head – for the rest of the body is covered in an overall . . . the mouth has no lips and resembles a hole . . .

These creatures communicated by a curious whistling sound.

If the extraterrestrial hypothesis is correct, and these strange visitors are the inhabitants of another planet, then two of their compatriots seem to have turned up in a suburb of Melbourne, Australia, in 1973. These creatures had some anomalous, ghost-like characteristics. They appeared *inside* the witness's room, apparently floating in mid-air. The witness described them as having large, bald heads, slit-like eyes, lipless mouths and small flat noses. One of the creatures opened its mouth and emitted a high-pitched whining sound.

The second type of creature that features regularly in abduction accounts is more human-like, taller than five feet. They are the creatures described by Betty and Barney Hill from their classic abduction. These beings, too, have distinctive eyes, usually described as 'oriental' or 'slanting'. Again, they tend to be exceptionally elongated, curving quite noticeably around the side of the face; again, noses or mouths are not prominent – in many accounts, such as Aveley, they are covered with masks or hoods. Their bodies are built to a more human proportion than the smaller creatures.

One small consistent detail is that both types of creatures often seem to have oddly webbed hands, sometimes with an irregular number (by human standards) of fingers. The Hills' captors, according to Betty, had only four fingers. A Californian abductee, John Hodge, revealed details of his experience in the early 1970s, under hypnosis. After an initial encounter with otherwise unrecorded 'brain-like' entities, Hodge is confronted by tall human-like creatures:

They are tall, skin grey . . . yellow eyes, very thin eyes, mouths but no lips, funny, flat noses. Their hands have long, thin fingers, six fingers and a thumb. They're webbed, more or less from the palm to the first knuckle . . .

The humanoid creatures seen by Betty Andreasson during her otherwise untypical abduction experience had only three fingers on each hand. It is details like these, repeated in case after case, in circumstances where it has been impossible for one witness to have known the details of another's experiences, that lend weight to the ETH and to the belief that perhaps two races of aliens are visiting this planet.

As well as descriptions of the creatures involved, witnesses' accounts of the alien craft into which they are taken also seem to demonstrate remarkable consistency:

This room is whitish. It's really big. It's curved on the inside . . . I don't think there are any angles in the room . . . everything is kind of milky or misty or something. It doesn't shine, but everything has almost that metallic glow to it . . .

This is part of the description of a witness identified as Steven Kilburn. It was given under hypnosis in 1978 and related to an incident that happened several years earlier, at an unspecified date. The witness, one of a number investigated by Budd Hopkins (see also Chapter Four), had no conscious memory of an abduction before the investigation. Kilburn was hypnotized to try to find the origin of a peculiar fear he had of a particular stretch of road.[31]

The absence of any direct source of light is another consistent feature of UFO interiors described by abductees. Charles Hickson, of the Pascagoula case, also reported that although the room in which he was examined by his captors had been brightly lit, there was no visible source of this light, which appeared to be 'all around him'.

Virginia Horton, another of the abductees investigated

by Hopkins, who seems to have been subjected to a double abduction and who still bore bodily scars from an operation apparently performed during an earlier childhood abduction, described her examination room as being filled with a 'soft gray' or 'pearly' light. One of the two youths involved in the Maine abduction described the interior of the craft in which he was held as having grey shiny walls, and no source of light.

The UFO phenomenon as a whole, of which the abductions are an important, but numerically small part, displays many features that seem to point to an extraterrestrial origin. There is nothing scientifically disreputable about this belief in the existence of intelligent races on other planets. Although the naive beliefs held by the early contactees about civilizations on other planets in our solar system have been totally discredited, as our knowledge has increased following the various space probes, most astronomers will admit that many varied forms of life probably exist on planets circling other stars. Indeed, some prominent astronomers have become involved with research programmes designed to seek out evidence for such extraterrestrial intelligence. However, they are attempting to do this by analyzing radio signals arriving from space, rather than by attempting direct contact via UFO occupants. Astronomers and biologists involved in 'SETI' (Search for Extraterrestrial Intelligence) programmes have argued that such life forms are likely to emerge on virtually any planet where the physical conditions would make it biologically possible. So the probable existence of some form of intelligent life elsewhere is not in serious dispute, even amongst the more cautious scientists.

But it *is* hotly disputed that any of these hypothetical civilizations has ever made the dauntingly long trek to Earth. Astronomers point to the enormous distances involved, and the lack of any convincing hard evidence. Proponents point to the weight of individual testimony of the many thousands of UFO witnesses. The abduction reports play a crucial role in this testimony.

Critics of the UFO phenomenon point to the dangers of misinterpretation and misperception of everyday occurrences, which may then become transformed into apparently marvellous and bizarre events. Many of the more serious UFO researchers accept this argument, and concede that only a very small percentage of all cases reported as UFOs can be said to have any validity as evidence for a new, genuinely unexplained phenomenon.

Allan Hendry was a full-time investigator for the Center for UFO Studies, a privately run investigation agency founded by J. Allen Hynek, former US Air Force astronomy consultant. During his tenure of this post Hendry investigated hundreds of UFO reports given to him, first hand, by witnesses. In his investigations he found an amazing degree of misinterpretation and exaggeration of quite normal events. One witness Hendry spoke to nearly battered down a neighbour's door to warn them of a UFO hovering nearby – on investigation Hendry identified the 'UFO', to the witness' satisfaction, as the Moon! Many other seemingly impressive cases, often reported by 'trained observers' such as police officers and airline pilots, also ended up with disappointingly mundane solutions.[30]

But the abduction cases represent a class of reports that cannot be misinterpretations of some other event. We can say with some certainty that the events described by abductees either must have had their origin in some very unusual physical event, or were *totally* imaginary – either hallucinations or hoaxes, whether perpetrated by the supposed witness, or played on the innocent witness by another person. Certainly, if a person reports being taken aboard a strangely constructed craft, undergoing a medical examination by exotic looking creatures, and returning home hours later, we are entitled to say, with some certainty, that this was no misinterpretation of the planet Venus seen through a heat haze! Consequently, the physical evidence for the abduction cases is crucial. If even one case can be found to have indisputable physical proof, then the 'ETH' is tremendously strengthened. But as we have seen in Chapter Four, this evidence is equivocal. Despite the unique nature of the abduction event, the final physical proof seems to be lacking.

So, again, we are left with the evidence of witnesses. We have seen how well many reports corroborate each other, and if this was the case for all reports – or even the great majority of them – the case for the ETH would be greatly strengthened. But although there is a strong 'family resemblance' between a great many cases, and although there are many uncanny details repeated in case after case, there is no final, overall consistency to all the cases which would suggest that there is some definitive explainable source for all these reports.

If we return to the story of 'P' and 'W', the two young men from Maine, we see that their experience tallies well with many other reports – the car-stoppage, 'missing time', strange behaviour of animals and wildlife, a medical examination with blood samples taken – the entities they met were described as having 'mushroom-shaped' heads, a feature which is not met with in any other abduction narrative we have on record. So is this a one-off, a single unprecedented visit to Earth by the inhabitants of a world who have not visited us before or since? If so, why do so many of the other details of their craft and method of operation seem to correspond so closely to so many other cases?

Betty Andreasson also reported many features of her experience that show a close resemblance to the general pattern. The examination room, for instance, is domed, has no corners, is suffused with a light from no visible source. There is an examination table, onto which she is 'floated', like so many other subjects of alien examination. All these features appear over and over again. But the rest of her remarkable tale is totally unique, and bears little resemblance to any other abduction or contact case reported to ufologists.

So, a search for patterns in abduction cases leads to an ambiguous result. We seem to find that many of the smaller details are consistent throughout the whole range of reported cases. Nearly all witnesses, for example, tell us that the dress of the entities seems to be seamless and without any apparent fastenings – our visitors apparently come from a planet ignorant of buttons or zips! But on the other hand many of the broad descriptions are almost totally inconsistent – in some cases, abductees have been told the name of the planet their abductors supposedly came from, but with a total lack of agreement.

It is true that, if the human brain becomes overloaded with unfamiliar, frightening and inexplicable stimuli it may, like some piece of machinery or electronics, 'sieze up' and go into a trauma. There are many cases of individuals who, having undergone some terrifying experience – a violent assault, a rape, seeing a loved one killed in an accident – are totally unable to recall anything of the incident. Others attempt unconsciously to alter their perception of the event so that they may cope more easily with what has befallen them. Yet others will fall into a deep state of shock in which they withdraw completely into themselves, avoiding all forms of contact with the outside world.

If a person actually had been forcibly captured by weird, alien creatures from another world, hauled bodily into their spacecraft, subjected to a scientific examination, and then dumped, hours later, dazed and baffled, this would surely be as disturbing and traumatic an event as any criminal assault or personal shock. It would hardly be surprising if, in these circumstances, witnesses' recollections of what had befallen them were erased from their consciousness. The reported 'loss of memory' and 'missing time' might as easily be a natural reaction to the terrifying events as a deliberate suggestion telepathically or hypnotically induced by the aliens.

Furthermore, an actual alien abduction would be something so unprecedented, so outside the realms of human experience, that it is quite possible that the human mind would be totally unable to understand anything that was happening to it at the time. The memories of this event would be confused and fragmentary. The brain constantly tries to create order out of chaos. We look for pattern everywhere, and feel uncomfortable when surrounded by disordered and unrelated effects. The fragments of memory that survived the trauma of a UFO abduction might then be woven together, producing a mixture of recalled fact and newly created fantasy.

If this should be the case, then it is likely that it will be the small, insignificant, but most familiar details that will be best remembered - the details of clothes, the construction of a door, the number of fingers on a hand. The larger, overall pattern would be so far beyond the percipient's comprehension that it could only be accepted if conventionalized into a more familiar scenario - a medical examination, or being shown images on a 'television' screen. It would be in this imagined scenario that the inconsistencies and the irrationalities would start to emerge. If the alien beings looked like nothing we had ever seen or could imagine before, we may as well 'remember' it as having a mushroom-shaped head as having a round head, as well 'remember' it as being three foot tall as being six foot tall. Its true form may well be something we could not - or would not wish to - describe.

But is it necessary to put forward such an elaborate theory just to smooth over some inconsistencies in witness descriptions? What is wrong with taking the witness's descriptions quite literally? Most of them seem to be averagely intelligent, articulate people, whose evidence we would accept in a court of law when a person's life or freedom might depend on it. If describing an accident or a bank-robbery they might mistake the colour of the car, but they would hardly be likely to confuse the get-away vehicle with an extraterrestrial spacecraft!

The trouble with this argument is that the descriptions,

taken at their face value, suggest that the Earth is not only being visited by a scientific expedition intent on studying the native fauna, but is playing unwitting host to a vast range of creatures from an equally vast number of alien worlds. Besides the two 'families' of creatures described earlier (the big-eyed dwarfs and the humanoids), there are creatures that have been described as 'moving jellies', totally human beings, the Maine Mushrooms, a whole flying-saucerful of small creatures looking remarkably like Kermit the Frog, and a bewildering variety of weird and wonderful individuals, including some that seem to have stepped from the pages of the more lurid comic-books. The different physical forms assumed by this menagerie necessarily mean that all these visitors must have evolved on different planets, where conditions suited each particular life-form. Yet in most cases these creatures have no difficulty in breathing our earthly atmosphere. As an exception to this we do have cases, like Antonio Villas Boas, where the humanoids wear some kind of breathing apparatus whilst outside the craft; yet once inside, these creatures, and the abducted human, are happily breathing the same air, and presumably the same micro-organisms!

Looking for alternatives to the ETH

These inconsistencies and irrationalities are so all-pervading amongst the abduction reports that it seem impossible to accept all the stories as *literal* descriptions of actual events, and even many of those ufologists who generally accept the ETH would accept this qualification. The question then becomes one of reconciling the apparent inconsistencies with the overall weight of evidence for the ETH. This problem has led to the formulation of a modified version of the ETH, which holds that extra-terrestrial intelligences are indeed responsible for the UFO abductions, as well as for a wide range of other UFO close encounter events, but that the wilder aspects of these cases are a result of direct intervention with the witnesses' perception, through manipulation of their brains and senses.

Indeed, a number of reports do seem to suggest that the abductors were directly interfering in some way with the minds of their human captives. The American UFO organization APRO (Aerial Phenomena Research Organization) investigated the case of a witness identified as Patty Price (not her real surname), whose strange experiences began just after she moved into a new home in a small mid-western town. Divorced, with seven children to look after, Patty woke up during the first night in the new home convinced that a prowler had been in the house. She took the children to a friend, and a neighbour called the police, but no one was apprehended. The next morning, discussing the incident, her seven-year-old daughter stunned her with the comment 'It wasn't a prowler, it was a spaceman!' Nothing could make her change her mind. About a year and a half later Patty read an article about UFOs in a popular magazine and wrote to find out more about her experience. The magazine passed her letter on to APRO, who began an investigation of the case under the direction of their representative Kevin Randle.[38]

Randle decided that hypnosis would be a suitable method for trying to find out what had happened that night, and while arranging for the services of a suitably qualified hypnotist, began preliminary investigation of the case, interviewing neighbours, checking police blotters and so forth. While talking to members of the family, he discovered that Keith, the youngest child, had woken up that night screaming and shouting that there was a skeleton in the corner of the living-room, where he had been sleeping. The seven-year-old who first claimed to have seen the 'spaceman' now told an elaborate tale of the spaceman and a spaceship. Although her mother discounted this as the child's imagination, the facts that Randle had uncovered convinced him to carry on with the regression as the best means of finding out what lay behind these events.

Mrs Price agreed to be interviewed by Dr James Harder, an APRO consultant who had handled similar cases for the organization. During the hypnotic session she began to tell what is by now a very familiar story, but with some rather intriguing differences. She remembered a bright light, then two figures, 'skinny' but human-like, wearing uniforms. Then she found that all her children were with her and several others of the uniformed creatures in a large round room, lined with computer-like machinery. In a second session Mrs Price described a medical examination she had been given by the aliens. She was laid on a table, hooked-up to a machine. Then a needle-like instrument had been put up to, or even *into* her head: 'They were taking my thoughts,' she said. 'They put a needle in and took my mind, my thoughts.'

In other hypnotic sessions conducted by Dr Harder, Patty went on to describe detailed accounts of her experience and of the creatures who captured her – including two completely human-looking people who appeared to be helping the others.

This report has some elements to suggest it might be a 'raw' abduction case. Perhaps the human-like and totally human creatures are the 'real' aliens, the many other conflicting descriptions being produced by the direct stimulation of the appropriate areas of the brain by the 'probe' which took Patty Price's thoughts. In many other cases we see a basic pattern of two types of creature, one more, one less, human in form. Could the 'probe' be the cause of the initial loss of memory in these cases, and could it also be the cause of the many conflicting recollections which other abductees 'remember' under hypnosis?

There might be two ways this could happen. The probe might be a deliberate method of implanting a false memory to provide a sort of 'cover story' by directly stimulating parts of the cerebral cortex. Alternatively, the induced memories might be mere side products of a process which, as Patty said, is 'taking' human thoughts, perhaps as part of a vast alien project to learn all there is to know about mankind.

This modified version of the ETH is able to deal quite well with some of the anomalies we have come across in examining individual cases. Besides explaining apparently irrational behaviour on the part of the captors, and inconsistencies of appearance in both the aliens and their craft and equipment, it also helps to explain why so few of the abduction cases have yielded any solid physical evidence.

However, critics have put forward some serious objections to this concept, pointing out that it is just *too* easy to explain any difficulties in a case as being the result of a 'space hoax', a deliberate invention by the aliens for their own ends. They say that *any* set of circumstances, however much they may seem to contradict the ETH, can be dismissed simply as an 'induced memory' by the aliens, and that the modified ETH cannot therefore be taken seriously as a scientific explanation. It is an axiom of science that any plausible theory must have within itself some way in which it *could* be proved false. To take an oversimplified example, the Laws of Gravity *could* be proved wrong if just one apple was shown to have fallen upwards off the tree! But there is no way in which the modified ETH could be proved wrong, because *any* anomalous circumstances – like our upward falling apple – can be explained away by simply saying that the aliens arranged it that way for their own unfathomable purpose.

The critics further ask if the mental processes that are alleged in the modified ETH could happen without the intervention of any visiting aliens – can the human mind unaided produce its own UFOs, aliens and abductions? Essential to any consideration of this question is an understanding of the process we call hypnosis.

Hypnosis – solution, or another problem?

The UFO abduction as a distinct phenomenon exists as a

result of the process of hypnotic regression. Although there are a number of cases in which percipients have been able to remember details of their experiences without the aid of hypnosis, the technique is used in the vast majority of cases. In some cases information is remembered without the aid of hypnosis; but in most of these it was an initial hypnotic session that seems to have triggered off subsequent, non-hypnotic recall. There are also cases in which the percipient remembers a few fragmentary episodes that are filled out in subsequent hypnotic sessions. So to a very great extent, the evidence for alien abductions stands or falls on the reliability of memories recalled through regression, and on the reliability of the techniques of hypnosis themselves.

There are many misconceptions current about hypnosis and what it does to the person 'under the influence' – a phrase which is itself a serious misconception, implying as it does some sort of psychic influence radiating from the hypnotist.

The techniques of hypnosis were first studied in the eighteenth century by Mesmer, who called it 'animal magnetism', believing that it was indeed an influence that pervaded all matter, analogous to magnetism or gravity. Mesmer even thought that this force was able to affect inanimate matter and experimented with iron rods and iron filings. Eventually, however, it became recognized that hypnotism was a psychological effect, which was largely the result of factors within the subject's own mind, helped along by the hypnotist. Most people will be familiar from stage or television performances of many of the methods used by hypnotists to induce a hypnotic state in their subjects – the swinging pendulum, concentration on a finger or bright light – and it is generally assumed that the hypnotist is placing his subject into some kind of 'altered state of consciousness', in which they are able to do or remember things that would be impossible for them in their normal state. But how true is this assumption? It is often thought that a hypnotized person is actually 'asleep' and unaware of their surroundings except the voice of the hypnotist; or, when aroused from the hypnotic state, that they are unable to remember anything they did or said whilst in it.

Experimenters have shown that some of the feats associated with the hypnotized state are easily reproduced by people without any sort of preparation. A common hypnotists' trick is to suggest to the subject that they will become rigid – 'a human plank' – and then suspend them between two chairs supported only by their head and feet. Often weights are placed on their body to demonstrate the rigidity which is supposed to have been induced. However, one researcher has compared this with similar attempts by non-hypnotized subjects, and has found no significant differences in the performance of this feat between both sets of people.[28]

Another researcher has investigated the accuracy of hypnotic regression for recalling details of incidents. A group of students were witnesses to a dramatic, but staged, 'accident'. A month later half the students were interviewed about the incident. The experimenters found that the accuracy of the non-hypnotized subjects was actually greater than of those students who were hypnotized.

Some medical experts are now coming to the view that there is no one state in which a person can be described as being 'hypnotized'; that hypnotism is something of a catch-all term for a whole range of different and well-known psychological phenomena. They feel that most of the cases of 'hypnotic recall' are simply the result of people being able to remember small details more easily in the sympathetic, calm and relaxed atmosphere of a psychiatrist's consulting room, or in their own homes, than in, say, a police interview room or a court of law, where there is a great deal more tension. Not surprisingly, therefore, many police forces have found hypnotic techniques – usually conducted by non-police personnel – to be helpful in allowing witnesses to recall details of crimes or accidents. The information recall is probably more a result of the *environment* in which the questioning takes place than any hypnotic 'influence' on the mind of the witness.

Of course hypnotists reject these arguments and present evidence that the process of hypnotism does produce some real change in the mental state of the subject, which is not reproducible in any other way. They point out that hypnotic subjects are more likely to perform uncharacteristic or pointless tasks whilst in a state of hypnotic suggestion, or are apparently more likely to be honest or truthful in replying to questions. This latter point is a vital aspect of hypnotic regression of alleged UFO abductees. Experiments by the American sociologist Milgram have shown that unhypnotized subjects are just as likely to perform uncharacteristic, even anti-social tasks whilst in a perfectly normal state, simply, apparently, to please an authoritarian 'experimenter' figure. He persuaded people, in a staged 'experiment', to administer electrical shocks to 'victims' who appeared to be crying in pain (in fact the 'victims' were actors, who felt nothing). There is a very strong desire amongst subjects in similar experiments not to 'rock the boat' and to give the experimenters what they think they want. This is done quite consciously, without any form of control, other than the normal social controls of 'politeness' or 'helpfulness'.

Similarly, experiments have shown that subjects are quite capable of lying through their teeth whilst in an hypnotically induced state. It would seem that the controversy over the value, or even the existence, of hypnotism will rage for a long time yet!

So where does this leave the ufologist confronted with the evidence for abductions gained via hypnotic regression? Is the abductee simply recalling additional details of his experience as a result of the quiet and sympathetic treatment he will receive at the hands of a skilled hypnotist; or is some previously blocked information being brought forward in an altered state of consciousness?

Two people who attempted to make some objective tests on the nature of abduction stories revealed through hypnosis are Alvin Lawson and William McCall. McCall is a doctor who practises medical hypnosis in his work and had been involved in hypnotic regressions. We encountered him as the hypnotist responsible for revealing much of the narrative in the 'Tujunga Canyon' cases in Chapter Three. He and Lawson (a professor of English) were anxious to find a way of distinguishing 'genuine' abduction cases from ones invented by the witness for whatever reasons, or were 'confabulated' during the hypnotic session – perhaps as a result of poorly designed questioning by the researchers, which might have led the subject's answers in a particular direction.

They began by locating a number of people who would be willing to participate in their experiments, but who knew little or nothing about UFOs – possibly a rather difficult task in Southern California where they operated, as critics later pointed out. These experimental subjects were then 'led into' a UFO abduction scenario by means of a carefully designed series of leading questions, which suggested the bare outlines of the abduction but left the subject free to fill in the details. These details would come, Lawson and McCall thought, from the witnesses' own imaginations. They would then be able to compare the imaginary abductions with the real events, and by a comparison of the differences between the two, would be able to gain valuable clues to use when trying to sort out any hoaxes in the cases that came to them as UFO researchers.

That was the theory. But the experiments went spectacularly wrong. In fact what happened was that the 'imaginary' stories were quite indistinguishable from the 'real' experiences, even down to tiny details. When the results of their experiments were released they caused a storm amongst American ufologists, who began to question Lawson and McCall's experimental techniques. Some argued that the UFO stereotype is now so well known amongst the general public that it was impossible to find anybody (especially in California) who was not already intimately acquainted with most of the details of the abduction phenomenon through reports, usually sensationalized, in the press and on television.

However, in some ways this criticism only served to strengthen the Lawson-McCall conclusion that there is no difference between the 'real' and the 'imaginary' cases. If the imaginary abductees have been exposed to UFO stories in great detail, so too have the 'real' abductees, and there may be no way to distinguish between their stories and accounts.

A very high proportion of the 'imaginary abductees', when asked to describe any beings they may have 'met' in their experience, came up with descriptions remarkably similar to the large-headed, large-eyed entities met by Travis Walton or Betty Andreasson. Others gave detailed descriptions of non-existent examination rooms, complete with table, instruments, and the strange, 'all round' light source that is a regular feature of the actual abduction reports.

After their first conclusions were published, the two researchers went on to put forward a radical new theory as to the origin of all these images. They argued that, as the same imagery was appearing in the 'real' and the 'imaginary' cases, then there must be some experience common to both sets of subjects that would account for these shared images. They claimed that what both groups shared was the most common human experience of all – that they were in effect reliving the physical and psychological traumas of the very moments of their birth.

As evidence, they pointed to the remarkable foetal appearance of most of the UFO entities – the outsize heads, disproportionate size of the eyes, the small arms and legs, even the 'webbed' hands – and the preoccupation in many abduction narratives with movement through narrow tubes and corridors, into rounded, womb-like internal spaces. The two researchers went on to compare the 'real' and 'imaginary' abduction descriptions with other reported experiences, including hallucinations produced through the therapeutic use of drugs like LSD. In an article in the British magazine *Magonia* introducing his 'Birth Trauma Hypothesis', Lawson sums up:

> [I have tried to show that] UFO 'abductees' unconsciously use major components of the birth process as a matrix for a fantasized abduction experience. Many parallels are obvious: the foetus, taken from warmth and comfort and subjected to prolonged distress in the birth 'tunnel', emerges into a strange world with bright lights, unconfined spaces, 'entities', an 'examination' and various sensory stimuli.
>
> Similarly abductees are levitated through a tunnel of light into a UFO's vast, brilliant interior where alien creatures examine and probe their bodies, often painfully. Additional parallels include such staples of CE-III [close encounter of the third kind] reports as a loss of time, absurd events, womb-like rooms, umbilical pain . . . The dominant entity type in both CE-III and Birth Trauma narratives is humanoid and closely resembles a foetus or embryo. The birth process is idiosyncratic and various so that no two CE-III narratives are ever exactly alike – though they are all very similar. Thus this research successfully explains how two different abduction victims can sometimes recall virtually identical experiences, and also accounts for minor inconsistencies among such narratives.[36]

Lawson and McCall claim that their hypothesis is falsifiable, a prerequisite of any truly scientific theory. If the abduction hypothesis was true, and the experience described is in fact a virtual re-enactment of the witnesses' own birth, then any unusual or particularly difficult births should give rise to significantly individualistic abduction narratives. For instance, a birth by Caesarian section should promote a narrative noticeably different from the norm, probably without the 'tube' or 'corridor' imagery which Lawson and McCall claim are memories of the birth canal. Initial investigations on a further set of

The prevalence of 'tube' and 'tunnel' images in UFO abductions may relate them to mystical experiences that present the same types of image. 'The Cave of the Mysteries', from Ebenezer Sibly's *Key to Physic* (1794).

'imaginary abductees' do seem to show such differences along the lines suggested. Subjects known to have been born by Caesarian section tended to describe their entry into and departure from the 'UFO' in sudden and dramatic terms: 'They threw me out', 'I was zapped out', etc. In one case involving a 'breech-birth', the subject reported being ejected from the UFO backwards. However, this confirmatory evidence is still limited in scope. Few attempts have been made to replicate Lawson's work, and it is difficult for an investigator, when attempting to study a 'genuine' abduction, to acquire sufficient knowledge of a witness's actual birth to be able to use it in any attempted analysis of their particular case.

Following the publication of the Lawson and McCall findings, critics have pointed out a number of further objections. The one that has attracted most comment is how it is possible for a foetus in the womb, even assuming it has a sensory system capable of forming memories, to obtain such an apparently detailed image of itself, enabling

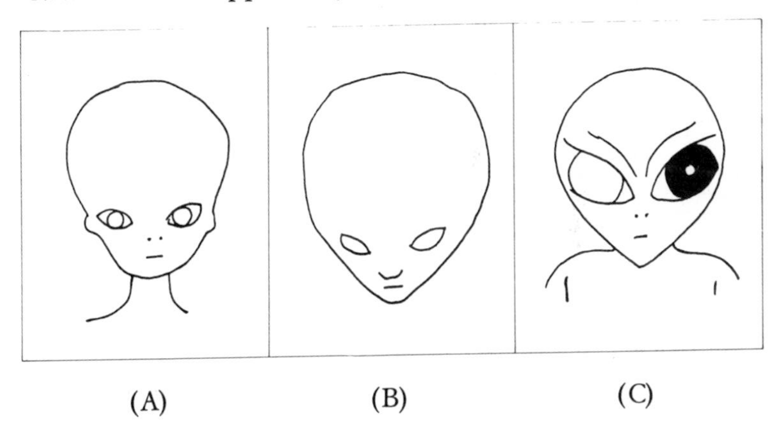

In his evidence for the Birth Trauma Hypothesis, Alvin Lawson compares the outlines and proportions of the head of the entity described by Travis Walton (A), the heads of Betty Andreasson's captors (C) and the head of a human foetus in its third month (B).

it to project this image on to imaginary entities in later life. Others have challenged the idea of the Birth Trauma itself, pointing out that the work of the psychiatrist Stanislav Grof, on whom Lawson based much of his reasoning, is not now generally accepted. Other critics have pointed out other possible sources for the 'foetal' entities, which, by the time Lawson commenced his work, was already a well-established stereotype, both in published UFO reports and in science fiction. On this latter point, defenders of the Birth Trauma hypothesis would argue that the reason the image was so widespread in the first place is that it strikes such a resonant chord in the human unconscious.[15]

Until more work is done which may corroborate or refute Lawson and McCall's finding, the hypothesis must remain an interesting and promising lead. It represents a hitherto unexamined possibility for serious research in a clearly defined area.

The psychological approach

Consideration of the Birth Trauma Hypothesis leads on to other explanations that put the question of abduction reports firmly into the category of psychological events with no external physical reality. This totally sceptical approach is spearheaded by a group of American critics who have made names for themselves by demolishing some of the better known American abduction, close encounter and UFO sighting reports.

This sceptical involvement in UFO research began in the 1950s, when atmospheric scientist Donald Menzel began offering mundane explanations of well-known cases of the period. More recently, aviation writer Philip Klass, James Oberg and Robert Schaeffer have proposed critical analyses of later UFO cases, including some of the well-known abductions. They have focused much of their criticism on what they see as sloppy investigation by many UFO proponents, who, they claim, fail to examine witnesses' statements with sufficient objectivity and are prone to gloss over evidence that may point to a mundane explanation for a particular sighting. They point out that on many occasions everyday phenomena can produce extraordinary reactions – we have seen examples of these from the work of Allan Hendry – and that the unexplained elements of UFO reports would not be at all mysterious if we had all the relevant information relating to a particular case. Often, they argue, researchers deliberately play down elements of a report that do not support their own particular pet theories. In a book that takes a sceptical look at a variety of UFO-related phenomena *(UFOs and Outer Space Mysteries)*, James Oberg points to the case of a hypnotically released abduction story in which one of the three percipients involved was actually shown drawings of alleged UFO entities whilst still in an extremely suggestible state. Obviously, subsequent descriptions presented by this witness will have been very seriously compromised by this act.[35, 44, 48]

But the sceptics themselves have also been accused of equally poor standards of research, by simply offering off-the-cuff debunking of cases, without themselves establishing the facts; and they in turn have been accused of fudging or covering up evidence that points to a non-mundane explanation. However, the critics do have a vital role to play in pressing for tighter standards of investigation in the whole field of ufology.

In recent years it has not been just the avowed sceptics who have begun to take a look at the possible psychological explanation for the abduction phenomenon and the UFO mystery generally. In the 1960s a number of ufologists in the USA and Britain became disillusioned by what they felt was the naivety of the extraterrestrial hypothesis, which they felt did not face up to the complexity of the reports they were investigating. Although increasingly doubtful of the ETH, they felt that the quality of the reported evidence was such that they could not adopt a totally sceptical approach. They soon attracted the tag of the 'New Ufology', although within that phrase there was a wide variety of approach. One of the leading figures in the movement was the Franco-American ufologist and computer scientist Jacques Vallée, who is said to be the model for the character of Lancome, the researcher in the film *Close Encounters of the Third Kind*. It was Vallée who first began to examine the links between ufology and folklore. Vallée has always been careful not to encourage too literal an explanation of his ideas; but broadly he sees the UFO phenomenon as part of a 'control system' which subtly influences mankind's development. However, he is reticent about the ultimate source of the 'control', and in his most recent book *Messengers of Deception* seems to be hinting that it is of earthly origin.[49, 50]

Another of the 'New Ufologists' was the American journalist John Keel. He again was instrumental in pointing out parallels between UFO experiences, particularly abduction reports, and folklore. In his later writings he moved towards a concept which he termed 'The Ultraterrestrials'. Keel sees the Ultraterrestrials as forms of electromagnetic energy, capable of almost infinite manipulation over the human environment. Although his books uncover a great deal of fascinating information, the Ultraterrestrial concept cannot be regarded as a serious scientific explanation of the UFO and abduction phenomena, for much the same reason as one is obliged to reject the 'modified' ETH – any phenomenon which is so infinitely manipulative is automatically beyond scientific consideration, since it could never be disproved. Even evidence pointing against the activities of the Ultraterrestrials could be claimed as proof for them – able to control everything, they can even control evidence which would hide their existence from inquisitive eyes! It must be said in fairness to Keel that much of his writing is rather tongue in cheek, and that he is more concerned with sparking off provocative and interesting ideas than with presenting a cut and dried explanation.[33]

A number of British researchers and writers grouped

around the small magazine *MUFOB* (originally *Merseyside UFO Bulletin*) began promoting 'New Ufology' ideas in this country in the early 1970s. Along with the American writer and editor Jerome Clark they moved towards a theory that found room for the purely psychological explanations of the hard line sceptics, but also realized that the phenomenon had many factors that could not be explained by the psychology of the individual witness. They accepted the 'universal' nature of the reports, but were influenced by the apparent lack of any conclusive solid evidence.

One of the few really great minds to examine the whole UFO phenomenon in any depth was the Swiss psycho-analyst Carl Jung. In an important, if little read, book called *Flying Saucers, A Modern Myth of Things Seen in the Sky*, he examined UFOs in the light of his own theories of the 'collective unconscious'. Jung proposed that the human mind, as a result of millenia of shared experiences amongst millions of individuals, has developed a common pattern of response to particular images. He called these images 'archetypes', and claimed that they were powerful symbols that provoked a universal response in people's unconscious minds. The UFO, he said, represented the archetype of the 'Mandala', a circular symbol of wholeness and unity. Some of the 'New Ufologists' were impressed by these ideas and began to integrate Jungian notions into ufology. They claimed that the events reported in the abduction stories were largely symbolic; that various unconscious concerns and preoccupations were being expressed in percipients' minds through a series of bizarre symbolic images. These formed a kind of 'performance', put on for the percipient's conscious mind by the unconscious mind, in order to express these concerns and fears. Just what these images might be is something which will be examined later.[32]

Like the Birth Trauma Hypothesis, this 'Jungian' concept has the great advantage that it seems to explain why the various abduction stories have so much in common, yet also allows for the individual details which vary from case to case – especially those details which seem to reflect some of the personal circumstances or preoccupations of the witness. On the other hand, like the 'Ultraterrestrial' explanations, it is perhaps *too* convenient for wrapping up loose ends, and because it attempts to explain one contentious subject (ufology) in terms of another (Jungian psychology) it could not be considered scientifically rigorous, and is probably non-falsifiable. Jerome Clark, who first presented the argument in detail in his book *The Unidentified* (co-authored with Loren Coleman),[11] began to move away from what he saw as some of its more naive features towards aspects of the study that dealt more directly with the physical manifestations of ufology. The English proponents tended to move towards more conventional psychological and sociological theories, whilst still accepting the fundamental validity of Jung's ideas on UFOs.

A distinction should be drawn here between the explanations offered by the out and out sceptics (or 'debunkers'), like Klass and Oberg, and the explanation of psychological theories being conducted by the 'New Ufologists' in the UK and particularly by a group of radical-thinking researchers who have arisen in France in the past few years.

The 'debunking' attitude is to look at each case in isolation and offer an explanation based on what can be deduced from the evidence that has been gathered for that particular case. If, after examining a case, they reach the conclusion that the witness's report is the result of an hallucination or delusion, or that there is insufficient evidence, other than the witness's testimony, to point to a definite conclusion, they consider that case closed and do not regard it as providing evidence for establishing any explanation for the abduction or UFO phenomenon. The 'New Ufologists', on the other hand, will still be interested in such a case. They will want to know why, given the seeming absence of any external cause, the witness reported what he did, and they will want to examine the psychological or sociological reasons why the percipient's report took the form it did.

A theory that proposes a psychological explanation for the abduction experience, whether considered in sceptical or 'New Ufological' terms, has at least one advantage over some of the others we have been considering. It is at least falsifiable – it needs only one piece of convincing, hard evidence for the extraterrestrial origin of just one UFO for it to be done; so, for the time being, the psychological explanations suffer, for most practical purposes, the disadvantages of so many others – the modified ETH or the 'Ultraterrestrials'; it is just *too* all-embracing, just a little *too* easy to explain away a potentially difficult case with an airy 'it's all in the mind!'

Each of the major theories put forward as possible explanations of the abduction phenomenon have aspects that provide a possible solution, some quite convincingly. Yet at the same time they have flaws that seem to prevent complete acceptance of them as a final solution. This fact in itself may well be a significant clue to the nature of the abduction experience.

SIX: THE MESSAGE OF THE ABDUCTIONS

The UFO phenomenon is building up to an official worldwide contact. This will occur immediately after a world war . . . The UFO contact will be made in order to sustain peace and will be the start of our acceptance as 'children of the galaxies'. The date will be about 1987.

In the early 1980s the Middle East will erupt. Israel will break off diplomatic ties with the US, and the Arabs will ally with the Soviet Union. Around 1982 Saudi Arabia will cut off the oil supply to the US and escalate the war. The actual fighting will be first between the Arabs and the Israelis, but will soon spread into the European bloc, and World War III will begin.

France and Italy will be hardest hit. The Soviet bloc will spread a limited missile bombardment around the East Coast of the US, but the missile-launched atomic warheads will not explode.

Widespread destruction will bring about fear on both sides that the entire Earth would be destroyed, and diplomatic relations will be reopened by 1984. By 1985 world commerce will be common. By 1987 the entire nuclear armaments of the US and Soviet Bloc will be disarmed. At that time official contact will be made by the UFOs.

One of the great unspoken fears of UFO investigators is that one day they, too, will see a UFO – or even worse, be abducted by one! Not that they are particularly frightened of what the UFO entities might do to them, for they must know that most people return from their experiences quite safe and sound. In fact, since they presumably know what to expect, they are probably less likely to be emotionally disturbed by such an event. But rather they fear that their credibility as a reliable investigator may be seriously compromised if they make such an experience public. For a start, critics will assume that they know enough about the details of such cases to be able to fabricate a convincing story. If they are able to demonstrate their sincerity, they will be held to be biased when investigating similar cases in the future, and their reputation as objective investigators may suffer.

The as-yet unfulfilled prophecies opening this chapter were presented to a UFO investigator, well known in California, when he himself underwent an abduction experience in August 1971. The case was investigated by researcher and writer Ann Druffel, who had known the 'victim' through her own work. Ms Druffel identified the chief protagonist in this event as 'John Hodges'. We have already looked briefly at this case when discussing the descriptions of UFO entities in Chapter Five.[17]

His adventure started when he and a friend, 'Peter Rodriguez', were visiting another friend at his apartment in Dapple Grey Lane (the report was published under the title 'Encounter on Dapple Grey Lane' in the magazine *Flying Saucer Review*) in the Santa Catalina area just south of Los Angeles. It was about 2 a.m. and the two men were getting into John's car, when they saw two strange objects on the roadway ahead of them. They were 'brain-like' objects, which seemed to be alive. Each was perhaps two or three feet high, with the surface convolutions reminiscent of a human brain. One was larger than the other, and this had a red patch on one side of it. Hodges drove Rodriguez home, driving past the objects, then drove home himself. He arrived back in his apartment at 4.30 a.m., but it was only later that he realized this meant that his short journey had taken two hours more than it should have done.

Years later, after he had been consulting Ann Druffel about UFOs seen over the nearby Santa Catalina Channel, he broached the subject of his conscious memories of this event. Ann arranged for a hypnotic session with William McCall, the hypnotist later involved in the 'imaginery abductee' experiments. The recall began with Hodges sitting in his car, alongside Rodriguez, just after leaving their friend. The 'brains' approached the car, and Hodges heard a message 'projected' into his mind by some sort of 'telepathy': 'We will meet again. Until then you will not remember what has happened here.' He drove Peter home, then went back to his own apartment, but while he was sitting in his car, about to get out, he had a vision of the entities again. Suddenly he was standing in a large room, alongside one of the 'brains'. Also in the room were several of the six-fingered humanoids described earlier. These individuals stood almost immobile, at a long console of instruments. At one end of this 'control panel' was a television screen.

The brain creatures spoke to him telepathically again, explaining that these humanoids monitor our world because 'there is too much power'. The screen shows pictures of parts of the world. There are pinpoints of light at locations where, it is explained, we could destroy ourselves – California, the US Mid-West, Europe, even places in the ocean. The screen now shows pictures of bombs exploding in deserts, on ice, or in the oceans. Then he was shown pictures of a dead planet, and told that this was caused by 'too much power'. His experience is over as suddenly as it began, and a moment later he was back sitting in his car.

It seems to be something of a pattern in two-witness abductions that the second person involved does not wish to be hypnotically regressed – we saw this with Aveley and Pascagoula – and at first Peter Rodriguez was similarly reluctant. However, he later consented, and in his regression account he confirmed Hodges' descriptions of the appearance and actions of the brain-entities that approached their car, although of course he was not present when Hodges had his principal experience later.

It was after the initial investigation, and just before a second hypnotic session was due to be conducted by Ann Druffel herself, that John met the strange creatures a second time, in 1978. He was suddenly 'transported' from his home back to the room. The two types of creatures were again present, but now it was explained to him that the humanoids are the intelligent creatures, the brains a sort of bio-enginered translation device. It was in this visitation that the messages concerning a coming world war were given to him.

When he was asked later about the curious prediction that atomic warheads unleashed on America would not explode, he explained that no nuclear warhead dropped from a height greater than 550 feet would explode, and that only ground-tested weapons will detonate. The bombs dropped on Japan in World War II were actually natural earthquakes; the US had sent out bombers with magnesium thermite to create a blinding flash, and had then scattered fissionable material around to create the impression of a nuclear explosion. No amount of argument seemed able to shake him out of his certainty of this bizarre belief.

Hodges went on to deliver further pronouncements about the aliens. He claimed that they had abducted thousands of humans, and implanted tiny, single-celled 'translators' into their brains (both he and Peter Rodriguez are claimed to have these), which allow psychic powers to blossom and give a new understanding of technical matters. The humanoid creatures are our 'cultural' ancestors, and were instrumental in helping the development of *homo sapiens* a million years ago.

A message in Mendoza

Do not fear . . . we have just made three journeys round your sun, studying customs and languages of the inhabitants of the system. The sun benignly nurtures the system; were it not so then the solar system would not exist.

A surprisingly banal message for representatives of an extraterrestrial civilization to cross the deeps of space to pass on to two bemused casino employees in a city in the Argentinian foothills of the Andes. But this is what we are led to believe happened at the beginning of September 1968.[7]

Carlos Peccinetti and Fernando José Villegas were driving home in the early hours of the morning from their job in the casino when their car stopped, and Villegas got out to investigate. As the other man stepped out to join him, they suddenly found themselves unable to move. Facing them were three humanoids, less than five feet tall, having large hairless heads and wearing overall-type outfits. Across the road on a piece of waste ground two similar creatures stood next to a hovering object about twelve feet across and five feet high, from which shone a powerful beam of light. The creatures approached the two men, seeming to walk on air as they crossed a drainage ditch at the side of the road. Then a voice sounded in their ears, as if from the ear-piece of a transistor radio. It delivered the message already quoted, ending with the statement 'mathematics is the universal language'.

Another of the little creatures started tracing peculiar designs, on the doors, windscreen and running board of the car, with a small device like a soldering iron. Then a circular 'screen' appeared in mid-air, which started to show a succession of images – a fertile country scene with a waterfall, then the mushroom cloud of an atomic explosion, then the waterfall again, but this time dried up in an arid landscape. Two of the humanoids took hold of the witnesses' left hands and pricked their fingers three times. Then they turned and walked back to the hovering object, and entered it by walking up the beam of light. There was an explosion, the object rose, surrounded by a 'vast radiance', then disappeared.

The two men, who were now able to move, rushed off to the local Military Academy, where after reporting their adventures to a bemused officer, they were sent off to hospital. Doctors who subsequently examined them did find small punctures on the left index and middle fingers of both men. Investigators who examined the car found the markings as described, but reported them as being indecipherable and unsystematic.

Although this account does not involve an abduction actually into the alien craft, nearly all the other elements of such accounts are present, even down to a rudimentary form of 'physical examination' – the puncturing of the men's fingers resemble many of the blood sampling features of actual abductions. When the men's story became local knowledge there was a considerable furore; but when this began to die down a remarkable thing happened – the two men publicly admitted that their story was a hoax, although it is not altogether clear whether they are claiming it was a hoax *by* them, or a hoax played *on* them. But it was probably not a coincidence that shortly before their retraction the police in Mendoza province, concerned by a wave of UFO reports and rumours, actually issued a warning that the spreading of stories about UFOs was likely to be penalized by law. The two men may well have decided that discretion was the better part of truth!

These abduction stories are different from the cold, clinical medical examinations of the Hills. They have more in common with the 'contactees' of the early years of flying saucers. But there is one very important difference. Although the message is the same one of brotherly love or warning, the creatures giving it are not the long-haired spacemen of the contactees but strange semi-human or even totally non-human creatures.

* * * *

There have been few full-blooded contactees in Britain,

but James Cook was one. He knew that he was going to be contacted by the space people, and he had often seen UFOs flying in the night sky above his home. This explains why he was standing out in a field in the middle of the night, next to the reservoir on top of a hill overlooking his home town of Runcorn, Cheshire. He was not to be disappointed. When the huge saucer came, it hovered just a few inches above the damp grass. A staircase descended from the craft and a voice told him to jump, not step, onto this gangway. The UFO, it seemed, did not operate properly in damp weather, and if he had 'earthed' the craft to the ground he might have received a nasty shock! Once inside he was surrounded by a light from nowhere, which cast no shadows. Unlike some of the abductees, Mr Cook was co-operative towards the tall (well over six foot) human-like entities he met there, and changed into a special suit they had ready for him – one, we note, which when put on appeared totally seamless.

Now he was taken off to the aliens' home planet – Zomdic, a name we meet nowhere before or since in UFO literature. Here he is shown many marvels and meets one of the 'wise men' of the planet, to hear this message:

Listen. The inhabitants of your planet will upset the balance if they persist in using force instead of harmony. Warn them of the danger.

Modestly, Mr Cook protests that they will not listen to him. 'Or anybody else', says the Wise One, with a sigh.

After having the mechanics of the spacecraft explained to him, in terms which make no scientific sense, Cook is returned to Earth where, forgetting the earlier admonition, he neglects to let go of the rail on the steps before touching the ground and receives a nasty burn. He had been taken up by the saucer at 2 a.m. on the morning of Saturday 7 September 1957. On his return it was 10.50 on the Sunday evening.[46]

Mr Cook's subsequent career did not achieve the

notoriety of Adamski or some of the other American contactees, but he did become a local figure in the Cheshire town. In subsequent years he kept up a 'psychic' communication with his space visitors, and opened a spiritualistic-type church, which grew large enough to generate another branch in the town and was featured in a Sunday paper exposé when its founder disappeared.

These preoccupations and warnings of self-inflicted doom are present in the messages given to John Avis during his abduction, and can be repeated over and over again in abductee and contactee cases from the 1950s to the present. They are all wise and timely messages, and had we the collective will to follow their advice, would doubtless lead to a safer and happier planet.

But before we thank the alien visitors for their concern, it would be as well to consider just how spectacularly obvious these little homilies are. An alien race that travels thousands of light years just to tell us, by means of simple illustrated allegory, that we are in danger of destroying ourselves in a planetary holocaust may have its heart in the right place (wherever that may be for an alien race), but it is hardly telling us anything that is not already being said more directly and more forcibly by newspapers and television bulletins every day. The alien's concern for our welfare seems poorly managed if all they can do is ask a Runcorn greengrocer to warn us of nuclear annihilation, then admit with a sigh that we wouldn't listen anyway. It is interesting and possibly significant that these warnings are invariably given to people who are probably least able to do anything concrete about them. Of the well-known abductees, about the only one who appears to have had any kind of public influence was Barney Hill, a civil rights worker and public figure in his home town (he represented Portsmouth, Massachussetts at Lyndon Johnson's presidential inauguration); but his particular case seems to have had no overt message at all – a wasted opportunity. The aliens' assessment of our level of scientific knowledge also seems rather off target, if they think anyone is going to be impressed by statements to the effect that the sun is an essential part of the solar system, or that nuclear weapons don't explode!

The overt message of the abductions is banal and commonplace. But it may yet take on a significance if we refuse to take the messages at their face value and look for the *covert* message which lies behind the abduction experience itself.

* * * *

Lee Parrish was a regular, all-American boy. Aged nineteen in 1977, he worked as a driver for his father's supply firm; a high school graduate, tall, well-built, well thought of, polite, intelligent, neat. At one o'clock in the morning of 27 January, in that year, Lee was driving home from his girl-friend's house in their home town of Prospect, Kentucky. As he drove a large shape appeared over trees a couple of hundred feet away from the side of the road. It glowed like the setting sun, but was perfectly rectangular in shape. The object seemed to draw his gaze and he could not look away from it, even though its brilliance hurt his eyes. By now he was very frightened; the car radio failed, and he felt that he had no control over the vehicle any more. He continued staring at the bright shape until he was nearly underneath it, when suddenly it sped away at tremendous speed.[47]

When Lee arrived home his mother commented on his eyes, which were bloodshot and painful. But he also noticed that the 7-minute drive from his girlfriend's had taken 45 minutes. Lee's mother contacted a local UFO group, who investigated the incident. Unlike many other UFO reports, the group was on the spot, and investigations began the very day of the sighting – an essential, but rarely achieved, prerequisite for a truly accurate investigation. At first Lee was concerned about what a hypnotic regression might involve, but after consultation he decided to go ahead, and the group began its investigation under the guidance of hypnotist Larry Allison.

The story continued from the first sighting of the glowing shape to when Lee's car arrived directly underneath it. Suddenly everything went black; the object turned black, then white. Now Lee could see nothing, but could feel something in his eyes. When he regained his sight he was in an all-white circular room, about twenty feet high and the same across – by now we hardly need to state that there was no visible source of light.

This much is typical, but now Lee's story becomes unique. There were no big-headed, silvery-suited entities with examination tables and instruments, just three large objects. To his left was a huge black slab-like object, as high as the ceiling of the room, with a rounded bulge protruding from the top. An articulated rod-like 'arm' reached out from its side. To Lee's right was a red object, the size and shape of a Coca-Cola vending machine, with a singular unarticulated arm or probe. Ahead of him was a white object, rectangular, about six feet high, with a square sloping protuberance on the top. The whole object glowed. The most remarkable thing about them was that Lee was convinced that each of the three featureless objects was alive and definitely aware of his presence.

The arm on the huge black object (or 'creature') reached out and touched him on his left side and back. It hurt. Lee thought that the red object touched him on his right shoulder and just above his ear. He felt a sudden pain, like a needle. After it had touched Lee the red object either moved behind, or merged with, the white one, which started making a rhythmic, scraping noise like pieces of sandpaper being rubbed together. The white object then moved towards the huge black 'creature', merging or disappearing behind it. Suddenly the black object disapeared too, leaving Lee standing alone in the white circular room.

In a moment he was back in his car and driving home. The following night he was telling the investigators what he knew about the objects: the white one was the 'leader', they were carrying out a physical check-up on him, checking his chemical make-up; they would be contacting him again.

The Lee Parrish abduction experience.

This is a unique case; we have no other report featuring such 'creatures', 'objects', 'machines', or whatever, although we do have a number of cases where abductees have been held by 'robots' or semi-intelligent machines under the control of humanoid creatures. But in the Lee Parrish case, the machine is in control not only of other machines but of a human being, plucked out seemingly at random, from the face of the Earth. In the story of Lee Parrish we are faced with a fear as widespread as atomic annihilation or environmental pollution – the fear of the technology which seems to be threatening mankind and has already deprived millions of their jobs. In other cases, abductees have described themselves being treated like laboratory specimens, subjected to blood tests, sperm tests, brain scans. With Lee Parrish his very body chemistry is analyzed; he is not even a laboratory rat, he is a specimen in a test tube – the dehumanization is completed in as clear and expressive an image as anything that could be devised in the world of science fiction to symbolize the fear of the advance of technology.

In this abduction there was no overt message, but the experience itself was the message, from whatever source it arose. So if we look again at the abduction reports, is there another message, built into *the events themselves*, that can perhaps be deciphered?

Seeing the light

Practically every abduction report we have begins with the percipient being surrounded by a brilliant light emanating from the UFO. Sometimes this is a beam of light that suddenly blazes out and almost blinds the witness. Sometimes the UFO itself is glowing, becoming brighter and brighter the nearer it gets.

In October 1974 a Buenos Aires builder, Gilberto Ciccioli, was awoken from his sleep just after three in the morning by noises coming from the front of his house – he thought it might have been his dog. As he approached the front door he was blinded by a brilliantly intense white light which came from no source that he could determine. The light made him lose all sense of time or place and plunged him into an experience which by now we can describe almost as well as he – the medical examination, blood and sperm samples, another loss of consciousness and the return. The only non-typical feature of Ciccioli's adventure is that he was able to remember these events *without* hypnotic regression.

The sudden eruption of a brilliant light just before some strange or abnormal event is not a phenomenon unique to ufology. It is something which has been described for hundreds if not thousands of years as the light of revelation; the light that has engulfed saints and mystics before their communion with angels, demons, the mystic teachers, or God himself. The light that blinds and dazzles the abductees is not the light that physicists know, the light that can be analyzed and assigned to its place in the electromagnetic spectrum.

The mystical light of revelation is a common feature of religious experience to the present day – 'seeing the light' is part of our language, and it is not just a metaphor. We have all read of the light that struck Saul on the road to Damascus. A great glowing light is the common prelude to reports of apparitions of the Virgin Mary or of the saints made by many thousands of pious people down the ages (see Kevin McClure *The Evidence for Visions of the Virgin Mary*).

This is the description by Richard Maurice Bucke, in his book *Cosmic Consciousness*, of one such revelation. Although he describes his own experience, he writes in the third person. Bucke and some friends had spent the evening reading poetry; at midnight he took a hansom cab home:

His [i.e. Bucke's] mind, deeply under the influence of the ideas, images and emotions called up by the reading and talk of the evening, was calm and peaceful. He was in a state of quiet, almost passive enjoyment. All at once, without a warning of any kind he found himself wrapped round as it were by a flame coloured cloud . . . the next he knew the light was within himself. Directly afterwards came upon him a sense of exultation . . . Into his brain streamed one momentarily lightning flash of the Brahmic splendour which has ever since lightened his life . . . He saw and knew that the Cosmos is not dead matter, but a living presence . . . that the universe is so built and ordered that without any peradventure all things work together for the good of each and all, and that the foundation principle of this world is what we call love . . . He claims to have learned more within the few seconds which the illumination lasted than in previous months or even years of study, and that he learned much that no study would ever have taught.[9]

There are a number of features of this description that are in close accord with descriptions of abduction experiences. Firstly, the mental state in which it occurs – quiet, almost passive enjoyment – the mind almost disengaged, quiet and comfortable. It would seem that this is a state that many people fall into when driving, often with tragic results. We note that many car-based abductees report that their first inkling that something is happening is when the car radio fades – which suggests that it had been tuned in to a music programme, thus contributing to the state of 'quiet enjoyment', especially on a lonely road at night when the demands of normal daytime driving may be reduced.

The comment that 'all things work together for the good of each and all' almost reflects the concern shown by the messages of the abductees.

At the moment of revelation, all knowledge is revealed to the percipient, and their life is changed. Gilberto Ciccioli's experience matches the revelation of Richard Bucke. According to the report that appeared in the British magazine *Flying Saucer Review*:

His intuitive sensitivity began to undergo an access of perceptivity hitherto unknown to him, and he began to possess knowledge – which he had previously not had – of the pure sciences such as Physics, Astronomy and Philosophy, subjects of which he had been utterly ignorant as a building construction labourer.

Ronnie Patrick was a builder too, living in the town of Tyler, Texas. In 1977 he became the subject of a series of peculiar experiences. Two shadow-like figures floated above the ground outside the door of his house in the middle of the night. On a subsequent night a silvery disc performed a series of aerobatic manoeuvres in front of him and another witness. Two years later he was working on a construction site when at 3 a.m. one morning he was woken by 'a beautiful beam of light' with 'sparkles' which entered his room through the wall. He touched the light and felt a tingling sensation. The next thing he could remember it was 7 a.m., and he was sitting, fully clothed, in a chair.

After this Patrick began to change. He claimed psychokinetic powers, alleging a Geller-like facility for bending metal and spoons. He also said he was able to name stars and constellations that he had never known before and had insights into spacecraft technology.[29]

The message of the shaman

There have been, in all ages and in all cultures, groups of people to whom the idea of a great blinding light as the herald of new knowledge and enlightenment is a part of their everyday life. They are the shamans, the 'medicine men' in tribal societies throughout the world. In the standard work on the subject, Mircea Eliade's *Shamanism*, the author quotes an account of the way in which an older master brings enlightenment to a disciple in the shamanic culture of the Igluik eskimos:

> Then the master obtains the angakoq for him . . . a mysterious light which the shaman suddenly feels in his body, inside his head, within the brain, an inexplicable searchlight, a luminous

fire which enables him to see in the dark, both literally and metaphorically speaking, for he can now, even with closed eyes, see through darkness and perceive things and coming events which are hidden from others; thus they look into the future and into the secrets of others.

In an even closer parallel to the abduction experience, the shaman, after his revelation with the blinding light, is taken upward into space. In many abduction experiences (for instance, those of truck driver Harry Joe Turner and Elaine Avis) the percipient is shown views of the Earth from space, or wonderful cities and landscapes of other worlds. So is the shaman:

It is as if the house in which he is suddenly rises; he sees far ahead of him, through mountains, exactly as if the Earth were one great plain, and his eyes could reach to the end of the Earth. Nothing is hidden from him any longer: not only can he see things far, far, away, but he can discover souls which are either kept concealed in far, strange lands, or have been taken up or down to the land of the dead.

Throughout abduction reports there is almost an obsession with light – the light initiating the experience, the beam of light through which entry to the UFO is often effected, the strange 'all round' light inside the UFO. Here, too, are parallels with the mystical experience of the shaman. In the course of his initiation he is 'bathed in light' or is 'surrounded by light'.

In the initiation visions of the shaman there is also a ritualized medical examination, but of a far more terrifying nature than anything experienced by the abductees – but even here there are uncanny similarities. Among some of the tribes of Australian Aborigines the shaman is sometimes visited by a supernatural being, who pierces the man's head then puts a magical stone into the wound. This gives the initiate secret knowledge and magical powers. Betty Andreasson and several of the abductees

In their ecstatic trance, tribal shamans seem to undergo many similar experiences to modern-day abductees. Shamans in Eastern Russia *c.*1850.

investigated by Budd Hopkins were subjected to some degree of pain during their examination, and at one point an instrument was pushed into their noses. They each felt that it had implanted something there, just as truck-driver Harry Joe Turner thought that his abductors had implanted a controlling mechanism into the left side of his body. The needle piercing Betty Hill's navel also seems to reflect the shamanic experience.

But more disturbingly, the shamanic initiation visions involve a ritual dismemberment – the body of the shaman is symbolically taken apart. In the legends of the Kiwai people of Papua the spirits of the dead would draw out a man's skeleton, replacing it with magical *oboro* bones. When he came back to the world of living men he would be an initiate, a magician.[19]

Sandy Larson was not a witch doctor from Papua, but a country and western singer from North Dakota. She and a companion underwent a time-loss experience in August 1979 during a drive from her home town of Fargo to the State capital at Bismark. In a subsequent hypnotic regression undertaken by Dr Leo Sprinkle, a professor of psychology who has taken a great deal of interest in UFO reports and abductions, she was questioned by UFO writer Jerome Clark. She described how the aliens 'opened her head' and 'took her brain out': 'It's like they wanted to connect something back different, when they put it back.'

Sprinkle's interest in abductions has prompted him to organize an annual conference at Laramie, Wyoming, at which abductees have spoken of and discussed their experiences. At this event the strong emotional response evinced by the abduction experience is apparent, and some observers have compared the event to a religious revival or crusade, with the abductees testifying, in almost religious terms, to their change or 'conversion' after the event.

Like the shaman of Siberia, or the 'witch-doctors' of the Australian Aborigines, the UFO abductees find themselves changed by their experience. Or the experience is a symptom of some deep-rooted psychic change that is already taking place in their life. After the event abductees become convinced that they have been *chosen* by the forces behind the abduction; that it was not just a random kidnapping on a lonely road. The UFO abduction is part of an experience that has a deep significance for the human mind, and the messages of the abductors seem to be the messages the abductees themselves want to spread. Afterwards, many see themselves as prophets or messengers helping to enlighten their fellow men and women.

So Betty Hill becomes a UFO cult leader, revealing to all who attend on her the space craft she sees wheeling and whirling in the cold winter skies of New Hampshire.

Charles Hickson, the Pascagoula abductee, becomes a prophet, preparing the world for the imminent coming of the aliens.

John and Elaine Avis become campaigners for a cleaner, healthier, more environmentally conscious way of life.

A message from our sponsors?

The ultimate message of the abductions may still be coming from the beings who are encountered in the strange craft that invade so many lives. But the message may not be what the creatures are *saying*, but in what they *are*. In case after case the abductees report that they encounter two types of entity. In the Aveley case there were the 'ski-suited' humanoids and the small, grotesque aliens; at Bebedouro there were the bearded dwarfs and the robed 'human'; PC Godfrey's 'Joseph' was accompanied by smaller, robot-like beings.

In purely psychological terms, these might be seen as representative of the conscious and the unconscious mind, the ego and the id. The humanoids are in control – at 'Dapple Grey Lane' they actually stand at a control panel – and they, perhaps, are the rational part of our mind, the part that makes the decisions which control our lives. These are the beings that give us the overt messages that we need to know in order to conduct our lives in a civilized manner: 'Be at Peace', 'The Sun [a metaphor perhaps for the rational, daylight world] nurtures the system'.

The other, more alien, more frightening creatures are then the hidden part of our nature. Elaine Avis's drawings of the 'examiners' depict an ape-like creature – a hint of our own animal origins – incongruous in a white lab-coat or surgeon's gown; just as our own irrational and animal nature is perhaps thinly covered by the veneer of civilization. These creatures are controlled by the humanoids, but when she was with them alone Elaine found them frightening – so can our own animal natures be threatening unless controlled by our conscious civilized minds. The 'robots' act mechanically, almost as if programmed to a specific task. In this they seem to reflect the mechanical, instinctive functions of our being, which again needs our consciousness, our own 'controller', to fit them into the delicate task of piloting an intergalactic spacecraft – Spaceship Earth itself.

SEVEN: SEARCHING FOR A CONCLUSION

What can be said with assurance about the abduction phenomenon? The evidence presented in this book allows us to put forward the following propositions:

* The abduction experience exists as something that is genuinely affecting hundreds, possibly thousands, of people. The number of reports that can be put down to hoaxes, played by or upon the witness, is tiny.

* The people experiencing abductions are sane, normal people, more or less a cross-section of society. Although we saw in Chapter Three some elements of personality or circumstance that seemed to be emphasized amongst the abductees, it is difficult, if not impossible, to identify an 'abductee type' before the event.

* The reports these people give us about their experience have a very high degree of internal consistency, and we can be certain that, with only a few exceptions, these people are all describing the same sort of event.

* On the other hand, each report seems to have certain distinctive features, which often seem to be reflective of the personality or circumstance of the witness.

In Chapter Five we looked at some of the explanations

investigators have put forward for the origin of the phenomenon. Although a number of possibilities have been looked at, when we draw up a final balance sheet, these all polarize into two options: the Extraterrestrial Hypothesis, and its various refinements; and the Psychological Hypothesis, with its variants. In the wider UFO field there is scope for a greater range of possibilities – misperceptions, atmospheric phenomena, etc; but the abduction experience is so explicitly reported that it seems to leave no room for wider interpretation.

The case for the Extraterrestrial Hypothesis

The case for the ETH can be summarized like this:

* We have agreed that the witnesses are sane, normal people by any reasonable standard. They are clearly reporting a series of frightening events that have occurred to them. We should be prepared to accept their testimony on almost anything else they told us, so we should be prepared to do the same on this subject as well.

* Reports from totally independent witnesses, who have no way of collaborating with each other, are identical in nearly all the major details of the experience, which strongly suggests a common physical origin.

* The experiences described by the abductees are consistent with the hypothetical activities of a group of visiting aliens conducting a scientific study of life forms on this planet. The existence of such aliens is entirely consistent with what we know of the structure of the universe and the development of sentient life.

* The entities involved in the abductions themselves tell us that they are extraterrestrials.

* The evidence from the wider UFO phenomenon adds weight to the ETH. The number of pieces of physical

evidence, multiple-witness and photographic cases in the UFO field generally point toward the presence of some actual physical, probably extraterrestrial, presence.

The case against the ETH

These are powerful arguments, and until quite recently have been accepted, almost without question, by UFO researchers, and by those members of the general public who have taken a sympathetic interest in the matter. But there are serious flaws in all these arguments, which have been pointed out by opponents of the ETH:

* The witnesses are indeed normal, sane people, but contrary to general opinion, normal, sane people are quite capable of gross misinterpretations of ordinary objects, and are liable, on rare occasions, to undergo quite elaborate 'hallucinations'; and of course abductions themselves *are* rare.

* Although reports are identical in many important respects, when individual details are studied there are as many different descriptions as witnesses. We have seen the amazing number of 'home planets' the humanoids claim to come from, and there is very little consistency in the details of the design and construction of the UFOs themselves.

* Many of the activities of the aliens do seem related to a form of scientific enquiry, but there are very many cases – e.g. Bebedouro, Andreasson – which seem far removed from scientific method and appear closer to the historical cases from folklore and legend. The behaviour of the entities is as frequently quite irrational as it is scientific. The arguments against such a wide variety of different civilizations visiting this small corner of the universe over a period of a few decades far outweigh arguments about the possibility of *some* intelligent life forms existing *somewhere* in the cosmos.

* The ufonauts tell us they are from other planets, but they never seem to agree on what planet it is. They also give us a lot of other messages which are misleading or downright untrue – the various 'prophecies' from the 'Dapple Grey Lane' case, for instance.

* The physical and photographic evidence which has been put forward to support the wider UFO phenomenon is as bitterly contested as that presented for the abductions; very few cases are universally accepted, even amongst ufologists sympathetic to the ETH. There is also a great deal of evidence which suggests that the abduction phenomenon is something separate from the general run of UFO events, and may have a different origin.

The case for the Psychological Hypothesis

So, can the arguments being put forward by some of the 'New Ufologists' justify ditching the ETH and supporting a purely psychological explanation for the phenomenon?

* The UFO abductions are part of a much wider range of myth and rumour that has formed part of human culture for thousands of years.

* The behaviour of the UFO entities is anthropomorphic – it reflects human preoccupations of the era; in our case, spaceflight, moonlandings, specimen-gathering, etc. The UFOs and their contents seem more like a projection of our own technology fifty or a hundred years into the future, rather than a genuine extra-terrestrial civilization that might be thousands of years further developed than ourselves.

* The phenomenon is culturally based. Most abduction cases come from North and South America, and Europe. Even within Europe cases seem centred on the UK. The only notable French case, the abduction of a young man

at Cergy-Pontoise, near Paris, is now shown to have been some kind of hoax.

* The messages of the entities conducting the abductions reflect the preoccupation of modern society – the Bomb, pollution, and even the curious preoccupation with sex. There are strong Freudian, and totally human, overtones to such cases as Betty Andreasson and Tujunga. There is the otherwise inexplicable predisposition for such events to occur to divorced, separated or unmarried women.

* The Birth Trauma Hypothesis provides a mechanism for the generation of reports. It explains their overall similarity, but also allows for the wide variety of individual detail personal to each witness. The nature of the hypnotic process itself also stimulates a significant part of each report.

The Case against the Psychological Hypothesis

These are arguments which have convinced a number of influential researchers, but they are still open to rebuttal:

* The abduction reports *are* similar to many myths and traditional beliefs. This is because the traditional stories are actually abductions, reported in terms that made sense to the societies in which they took place. Consequently, they were interpreted in terms of gods, demons, etc. However, the descriptions of the entities and their activities were basically accurate, and we now find that they broadly correspond with modern abduction reports.

* The entities' behaviour is anthropomorphic because civilizations that have developed space-flight, and are using it for scientific enquiry, are likely to have much the same sort of motives and methods as ourselves. Witnesses are likely to take more notice of activities

they find understandable, and ignore those aspects of the aliens' work they find totally baffling.

* It is the *reporting* of the abductions that is culturally based. North America, South America and Europe have a vast range of press and media outlets, many of which are sympathetic to sensationalized stories of UFOs and the like. Much of the 'Third World' has state-controlled media, which are much less open to such news items. Communications in these countries are poorer, and abductions taking place in remote parts of these countries may never be heard of in the cities where the newspapers and broadcasting organizations are based.

* It is not surprising that our visitors should warn us about possible disasters in store for us. As an advanced and widely travelled race they may well have seen other civilizations destroying themselves as we are threatening to do. Their concern need be no more than a sense of altruism. Nor is it surprising that beings conducting a scientific study should be particularly interested in our sex life. Human scientists have studied the sex life of the liver-fluke; we should not be surprised at extra-terrestrial visitors showing a similar interest in the predominant species on Earth.

* The Birth Trauma Hypothesis is far from being proved, and is challenged by many experienced researchers. Even the existence of any form of birth trauma is a subject of considerable controversy amongst psychologists themselves.

* * * *

Before any final statement on the abduction phenomenon can be made, some extra evidence is needed. Until then any statements must be entirely personal, and can only be considered provisional and tempered with belief as well as proof. Some of the new evidence that would be needed to clinch the matter one way or the other might include:

* The finding, or presentation, of an extraterrestrial artefact that would be available for long term scientific examination, preferably by several independent groups of researchers. Even if this artefact came from a non-abduction case, such physical evidence of extraterrestrial intervention would immeasurably strengthen the arguments for extraterrestrial abductions.

* A UFO landing or abduction incident, witnessed by several independent witnesses, physically separated from each other, all of whom would have to be interviewed before having *any* contact with the others. Independent movie-film evidence would probably clinch the matter. However, under some circumstances even this would not rule out the possibility of a large-scale hoax.

* The proverbial mass landings in Hyde Park.

* The psychological theories would be greatly strengthened by the presentation of a theory that could be experimentally tested – in effect, by producing abduction reports, identical in all respects to the 'real' reports, virtually to order. The Birth Trauma Hypothesis may indicate a line of experiment, but it cannot yet be said to be proven.

* By finding witnesses to percipients in hallucinatory states whilst undergoing abduction experiences. For instance, discovering a policeman who stopped by the Avis's stalled car at Aveley and saw the family apparently asleep inside, or an independent witness passing by the pier at Pascagoula who saw Hickson and Palmer perhaps lying unconscious. But even here we are back to the question of one individual's testimony.

EIGHT: A PERSONAL ASSESSMENT

I shall conclude this survey with what must be a series of entirely personal statements. I *believe* that they are borne out by the evidence I have presented; but I am aware that they are open to argument and denial, until and unless some form of final proof is presented. I think we shall have a very long wait for this!

* The flaws in the ETH are, in my view, fatal. The absence of indisputable physical evidence alone would be enough to cast the most serious doubts over the hypothesis. Ufologists have seen, one by one, many of the best examples of physical or photographic evidence fall as better analytical techniques have been employed, or more has been found out about the background to individual cases.

* Although there are some individual cases of UFO sightings that seem hard to explain, taken as a whole these cases do not seem to be different in kind from the overwhelming majority of such reports that *have* been explained. They seem to belong to the same class of phenomena.

* The abduction reports seem to be rather different from the more general range of UFO reports. The experience appears to reflect something of the person reporting it,

unlike many other types of UFO sightings, which are of a more objective character. Even so, many 'ordinary' UFO reports also show this 'personal' factor, which would suggest that many of them also have a psychological explanation.

* The content of the abduction story is personal to the individual recounting it and is based on their own background and condition. But abduction reports also show a symbolism that is based on ideas and images understandable to all of us. This explains the emotional force of many abduction narratives.

* The abduction stories form a continuum with old legends and beliefs. These are not distorted memories of 'ancient astronauts', but can be shown to be an integral part of the culture of the period, growing out of the entire social framework of the time. Similarly, the modern abduction cases grow from our own cultural and social background and reflect our own fears and preoccupations, both on a personal level, with worries over sex, status and security, or on a social level, with concern over pollution, the survival of mankind, and the potential threat of scientific development.

* All these considerations lead me to conclude that the abduction experience is almost totally psychological in origin, and individual cases can be explained without recourse to extraterrestrial intervention. The original stimulus that triggers off the psychological process in many cases seems to be some form of personal crisis, and the abduction is a symptom, rather than the cause, of a change in attitude or lifestyle. In some cases there may be a physical stimulus that initiates the psychological process – direct stimulation of the cerebral cortex by a natural electrical phenomenon has been suggested; but although this is possible, I do not believe it to be an essential part of the phenomenon.

* The Birth Trauma Hypothesis presents one of the most potentially fruitful lines for future research. Even if it does not provide a definitive answer, it is important for opening up the question of the nature of the hypnotic evidence.

* Above all, I am quite sure that the abduction reports are important. They do contain a message, and I believe it is a message about ourselves and the kind of world we live in. It is a message put forward by a growing number of people who have perhaps no other way of expressing the anxieties and crises of their lives – people in the main like us. It is a message given to us by the hidden parts of our being, and it is a message we should listen to carefully.

BIBLIOGRAPHY AND SOURCES

This bibliography serves as an indication of the published sources on which this book is based and as a guide to further reading.

1. Aleixo, Hulvio Brant, 'Abduction at Bebedouro', in *Flying Saucer Review*, vol.19, no.6, November 1973.
2. *APRO Bulletin*, vol.31, no.1.
3. Barry, Bill, *Ultimate Encounter*, Corgi, 1981.
4. Basterfield, Keith, *Close Encounters of an Australian Kind*, Reed, Sydney, 1981.
5. Boédec, Jean-Francois, *Fantastiques Rencontres au bout du Monde*, Le Signor, Quimper, 1982.
6. Bowen, Charles (ed.), *The Humanoids*, Neville Spearman, 1969.
7. Bowen, Charles, 'One Day in Mendoza', in *Flying Saucer Review,* vol.14, no.6, November 1968.
8. Bowen, Charles, *et al*, 'A Significant Report from France', in *Flying Saucer Review*, vol.19, no.5, September 1965, *et seq*.
9. Bucke, Richard Maurice, *Cosmic Consciousness*, Innes, Philadelphia, 1905.
10. Creighton, G. (ed. and tr.), 'The Most Amazing Case of All', in *Flying Saucer Review*, vol.11, no.1, January 1965, *et seq*.
11. Clarke, Jerome, and Coleman, Loren, *The Unidentified*, Warner, New York, 1975.
12. Collins, Andrew, 'The Aveley Abduction', in *Flying Saucer Review*, vol.23, no.6, April 1978, and vol.24, no.1, June 1978.

13. Collins, Andrew, *The Supernaturalist*, Parasearch, Essex, 1981.
14. Condon, Edward U., *Final Report of the Scientific Study of Unidentified Flying Objects*, University of Colorado, 1968.
15. Cresswell, Ian S., 'Objections to the "BT" Hypothesis', in *Magonia*, no.11, 1982.
16. Creighton, G. (comp.), 'A New FSR Catalogue: the effects of UFOs on animals, birds and smaller creatures', in *Flying Saucer Review*, vol.16, no.1, January 1970, *et seq.*
17. Druffel, Ann, 'Encounter on Dapple Grey Lane', in *Flying Saucer Review*, vol.23, no.1, June 1977, and vol.23, no.2, August 1977.
18. Druffel, Ann, and Rogo, D. Scott, *The Tujunga Canyon Contacts*, Prentice Hall, New Jersey, 1980.
19. Eliade, Mircea, *Shamanism; archaic techniques of ecstasy*, Routledge, 1964.
20. Fickett, Sheila M., 'Maine UFO Encounter'; Raynes, Brent M., 'Twilight Side of a UFO Encounter'; Schwarz, B. E., 'Psychiatric-paranormal aspects of the Maine Encounter', all in *Flying Saucer Review*, vol.22, no.2, July 1976.
21. Fowler, Raymond E., *The Andreasson Affair*, Prentice Hall, New Jersey, 1979.
22. *Frontiers of Science*, vol.3, no.2, January 1981.
23. Fuller, John G., *The Interrupted Journey*, Dial, NY, 1966.
24. Gansberg, Judith and Alan, *Direct Encounters*, Walker, NY, 1980.
25. Hall, Richard, *UFO Evidence*, NICAP, Washington DC, 1964.
26. Hartland, Edwin, *The Science of Fairy Tales*, Methuen, 1925 (2nd. ed.).
27. Heiden, Richard, 'Pascagoula UFO and Occupant Incident', in *Flying Saucer Review*, vol.20, no.6, April 1975.
28. Hearne, Keith, 'A Cool Look at Nothing Special', in *Nursing Mirror*, 20 January 1982; quoted in *Common Ground*, no.4, February 1982.
29. Hendry, Allan, 'Abducted!', in *Frontiers of Science*, vol.2, no.5, July 1980.
30. Hendry, Allan, *The UFO Handbook*, Doubleday, NY, 1979.
31. Hopkins, Budd, *Missing Time: a documented study of UFO abductions*, Marek, NY, 1981.
32. Jung, Carl Gustav, *Flying Saucers: a modern myth of things seen in*

the sky, Routledge and Kegan Paul, 1959.
33. Keel, John, *The Eighth Tower*, Dutton, NY, 1976.
34. Keyhoe, Donald, *Flying Saucers are Real*, Fawcett, NY, 1950.
35. Klass, Philip J., *UFOs Explained*, Random House, NY, 1974.
36. Lawson, Alvin, 'The Abduction Experience - a testable hypothesis', in *Magonia*, no.10, 1982.
37. Leslie, Desmond, with Adamski, George, *Flying Saucers have Landed*, Werner Laurie, 1953.
38. Lorenzen, Coral and Jim, *Abducted!; confrontations with beings from outer space*, Berkley Medallion, NY, 1977.
39. *Malaysian UFO Bulletin*, no.4, April 1982.
40. Maple, Eric, *The Dark World of Witches*, Hale, 1962.
41. Métraux, Alfred, *Voodoo*, Deutsch, 1959.
42. Michel, Aimé, *Flying Saucers and the Straight Line Mystery*, Criterion, NY, 1958.
43. Morin, Edgar, *Rumour in Orleans*, Blond, 1971.
44. Oberg, James, *UFOs and Outer Space Mysteries*, Downing, Norfolk, 1982.
45. Randles, Jenny, 'A Policeman's Lot', in *Flying Saucer Review*, vol. 22, no.2, August 1980.
46. Roberts, Thelma, *Flying Saucer Review*, vol.3, no.3, May 1955.
47. Rueckert, Carla L., 'Kentucky Close Encounter', in *Flying Saucer Review*, vol.23, no.3, October 1977.
48. Schaeffer, Robert, *The UFO Verdict*, Prometheus, NY, 1981.
49. Vallée, Jacques, *Messengers of Deception*, And/Or Press, Calif., 1979.
50. Vallée, Jacques, *Passport to Magonia*, Regnery, Chicago, 1969.
51. Van Vlierden, 'Escorted by UFOs from Umvuma to Beit Bridge', in *Flying Saucer Review*, vol.21, no.2, August 1975.
52. Wentz, W. Y. Evans, *The Fairy Faith in Celtic Countries*, OUP, 1911.
53. Zinstag, Lou, and Good, Timothy, *George Adamski, the Untold Story*, CETI Publications, Beckenham, 1983.

INDEX

§ indicates that the person named is an abductee.
*Cases marked * contain information revealed through hypnotic regression.*